Making the Most
of Your First Job

Making the Most of Your First Job

by the Staff of Catalyst

G. P. Putnam's Sons
New York

Catalyst gratefully acknowledges permission to quote lyrics from "Can't Buy Me
Love," Copyright © 1964 Northern Songs Ltd. All rights for the U.S.A., Mexico
and the Philippines controlled by Maclen Music, Inc., and Unart Music
Corporation. All rights reserved.

Library of Congress Cataloging in Publication Data

Catalyst, inc.
Making the most of your first job.

Bibliography: p.
1. Vocational guidance for women.
2. Résumés (Employment)
3. Employment interviewing.
I. Title.
HF5381.C396 1981   650.1'4'024042   80-25001
ISBN 0-399-12609-0

Designed by Bernard Schleifer

Printed in the United States of America

ACKNOWLEDGMENTS

2148760

CATALYST gives warm thanks to the Weyerhaeuser Company Foundation for providing the funding for this book. Their generous support clearly demonstrates their commitment to the full participation of women in the work force in a manner that is maximally productive for both women and employers.

CONTRIBUTORS

The staff of Catalyst conceived and executed the research, writing and editing of this book.

The publications staff includes Elizabeth A. Niles, managing editor; Larayne Gordon, senior editor; Maria L. Muniz, editor; and Amanda Linn, assistant. This book was edited by Carol Day. Writers were Maria L. Muniz and Charlotte Knabel. Gail Fleckner and Diane Salino assisted with the research.

We would like to give special thanks to the reviewers, advisers, and experts who contributed their expertise and support to our efforts. During the course of our interviewing, many people gave us information that was confidential, in the hope that it might help others with similar problems. Therefore, as they used to say, approximately, on an old police show, the stories you are about to read are true but the names have been changed to protect the innocent. All "first-jobbers" quoted will remain anonymous—they have enough to worry about without the added "notoriety" of appearing in a book. Finally, to everyone, acknowledged and anonymous, who gave so willingly of their time, advice, experiences, and most of all, encouragement—our sincerest thanks.

CONTENTS

Queen Bee or Kindred Spirit: Working for a Woman

> Attention: Working Mothers

Part III: Skills and Strategies, or Learning What Everyone Assumes You Already Know

> Time Tips from the Pros. Time Tips from Some Nonpros. How Can You Manage Home and Job? Time Tips for the Harried Homemaker

> Help for the Tongue- and Pen-Tied. Advice for the Shy, the Meek, and the Intimidated

Know Your Rights

Credit Quiz. Married Women's Credit Rights. If You Can't Pay the Bill Collector. Danger Signals. Consumer Credit Laws

Part IV: Looking Back, Looking Ahead

> Collecting Credentials

> What to Do When You're Fired or Laid Off

PREFACE:
CATALYST—WHAT IT IS;
WHY WE WROTE THIS BOOK

CATALYST: Something that brings about a change, that initiates a reaction and enables it to take place. Catalyst, the national nonprofit organization dedicated to expanding career and family options for women, has been pioneering new inroads for the working woman since it was founded in 1962 by its president, Felice N. Schwartz, and five college presidents. Today, with a staff of thirty full-time professionals and long-standing contacts in the corporate and professional community, Catalyst has a comprehensive national program that:

- Informs women, employers, counselors, educators, legislators, and the media about issues of common interest through its multimedia information center, open to the public.
- Offers career information and guidance to women at all stages of their careers through its books, filmstrips, videotapes, and career series.
- Provides counseling to nearly one million women through its network of more than 200 affiliated resource centers nationwide.

- Helps corporate women advance in their careers, and helps employers respond to their needs through special programs.
- Offers corporations outstanding women candidates for corporate directorships and assists them with their search through its Corporate Board Resource.
- Addresses the specific needs and problems of two-career families and their employers through the Career and Family Center.

Catalyst's current priorities include addressing the needs of the undergraduate woman, the upwardly mobile woman, and the two-career family. Our role is to facilitate the growing partnership of employers and women by helping women plan and develop their careers, and by helping business and industry identify and develop the talent and leadership they need.

INTRODUCTION:
THREE "CINDERELLAS"—
A NEW TWIST ON AN
OLD STORY

ONCE UPON A TIME—not so long ago—Cinderella One graduated from college and went to work as a secretary or an administrative something-or-other. She typed a lot and waited for Prince Charming to appear. When the Prince did come along, she quit her job; they got married and had two children. And they lived happily ever after. (Everyone knows that fairy tales always have happy endings.)

Once upon another time—fairly recently—Cinderella Two graduated from college and got her first job. She was a bit apprehensive: she wasn't certain she could handle it. Although Cinderella had never even typed, she quickly learned all about organizational hierarchies, mentors, office politics, getting a raise, writing memos, and planning her career. She made a few mistakes along the way, but she learned a lot from them. When the Prince came along this time, he didn't win her over. Instead he began to compete with her for the boss's attention—and for a promotion Cinderella Two wanted. But Cinderella Two got the promotion, and . . . well, we don't really know whether she lived happily ever after or not. After all, this wasn't a fairy tale.

Once upon a time, Cinderella Three spent twelve years at home in the castle—cooking, cleaning, and caring for her family. It came to pass, however, that the Prince's income was no longer enough to keep up with the rising costs of maintaining the family and the castle. Cinderella was also getting itchy to do something different for a change. So she decided it was time to return to the paid work force. She was excited, but also scared. Cinderella felt unsure about her ability to handle a job; after all, she'd been away from the paid labor force for some time. She'd have to relearn many things about the world of work, and make many adjustments. Cinderella experienced many of the same problems that "younger" first-jobbers were having, but she learned from all her mistakes—and successes. And, with the help of the Prince and her family (everybody had to pitch in and take on more responsibility), Cinderella was able to manage. Although we're not sure if Cinderella (and her family) will live happily ever after, she and the Prince and the kids are working on it, and they seem to be doing OK—they certainly are busy!

Welcome to the real world, all you modern Cinderellas.

Part I

Work-World Realities, or What Your Education Never Taught You

THE START OF
SOMETHING BIG

1

YOU GET THE JOB—the one you really wanted—and, elatedly, you accept it. It will be your first professional position, the beginning of your career. You go to bed dreaming of the day when you will be made chair of the board. The next morning, however, you don't feel as elated. In fact, you're pretty nervous. You start to speculate: Suppose I can't handle the job? I've had little or no experience working in a "real" office before—how am I going to know what to do? Is this *the* right job for me? Suppose I've made a BIG MISTAKE?

If you've already begun your first job, maybe things aren't going as smoothly as you thought they would. You're not sure what's expected of you. Everyone around the office seems like an old pro, and all of a sudden you're feeling very young and inexperienced.

If you're still in school, you're probably wondering what *is* "out there"—what's it like to start a career, work at your first job?

And if you're a woman entering (or reentering) the paid labor force after having been home for several years, you're probably also worried about being able to juggle mother, wife, and job responsibilities.

Welcome to the club. Out there, hundreds of women like yourself are just as apprehensive. Although school may have taught you everything from Brownian movement to Beckett, there's one thing it didn't teach you—how to make the school-to-work transition painlessly.

Whether your professors may believe it or not, there's a world outside the proverbial ivory tower; it's full of people whose lives do not revolve around existential philosophers or metaphysical poetry. Out there is a workplace with its own unique culture, customs, rules, and regulations. Your first job will be your introduction to this "alien environment."

Basically, we wrote this book because, as Harvard professor Anthony Athos noted, "It has become increasingly recognized that the first year on the job for college graduates is often a discouraging, cold-shower introduction to the real world." While this book was written primarily with the "younger" first-jobber in mind, many of the problems faced in making the transition into the work world are similar—whether you're twenty-one, thirty-one, or forty-one. (For all you Cinderella Threes: There are some sidebars written especially for you.)

We can't promise to prepare you for any and every situation you will encounter on the job. But by enabling you to share the experiences of people who have survived the transition, we hope to take some of the sting out of that cold-shower introduction. Take heart; beginnings are always stressful, but they are also exciting, revealing, and fun. Your first job should be no exception.

Why Your First Job Is So Important

How important is that first job? Our interviewees gave us some of these replies:

"The first job may be the most important job a woman ever has; it begins to create the image a woman has of herself as a professional."

"My first job was crucial for me; it contributed to making me the person I am now."

"I think the first job is critical. As a matter of fact, if I had had a very bad experience at my first job, I might have decided to switch careers."

"The first job one has is extremely important. You discover during your first job what kind of a person you like to have as a boss, and what kind of an environment allows you to be the most comfortable. You also start to get an idea of money—of what you are worth. It's an important basis for your next job."

Your first job lays the groundwork on which you will build your career. The first year at work is almost like serving an apprenticeship, in that most of what you will need to know as a worker will be learned on the job. The company is, in effect, paying you to be a "student" once more.

On your first job you will begin to learn all the technical and nontechnical skills that you will need for any job—from learning the ins and outs of writing memos and business reports to developing the interpersonal skills that are crucial in dealing effectively with a wide variety of people.

You will also get the exposure that will enable you to develop your first business contacts. Not only will you be observing those around you, but people will be looking at you to see what you can do. You will meet people both inside and outside your organization who can help you move up in your first job, or get your second or third—or tenth!—job. You will begin to develop your own network of people on whom you can rely for information, advice, or maybe just an encouraging pat on the back when you need it.

For novice workers still largely unsure of their abilities, the first job can be an important boost to their self-confidence. "Confidence," says (Ms.) Michael Kraft, a director of sales personnel development at the New York Life Insurance Company, "comes when you've had enough experience and enough association and interaction with other people. That way, you have benchmarks. You can say, 'Well, I know I'm better than that,' or 'I'm not quite that good yet; here's someone I think is about the same as I am.' You have to have contact before you can peg yourself."

Another bonus the first job offers is your first opportunity to get an inside view of a career field. It's one thing to read about a profession, quite another actually to be a part of it. That first position can help measure your aptitude and interest in a particular career.

Perhaps most importantly, the job will help you begin to develop a broader view of the way people and organizations function. By observing the successes and mistakes of others, you will start to develop a style of your own.

"A woman can gain initial insights and learn one pattern from her immediate company," says Judith Warner of Consolidated Edison, a utility company, "and begin to compare and contrast it with other situations she hears about. I think she should watch to see how people who are actually successful achieved it . . . if you see that X is successful, you can say to yourself: 'Is there a certain way X handles people, and do I want to do it the same way? If I can't, how can I bring my own treatment to a similar situation?'"

Why Your First Job Isn't So Important

Obviously, your first job is important in lots of ways. But on the other hand, despite what we just said, let us also say this: Your first job may not be that important.

Many new workers approach their first jobs as if they were walking to the gallows. "This is it," they say. "If I don't make it here, I'm really done for." Well, there's no need to feel as if you have to make *the decision* at this point. That your first job will determine the course of the rest of your life is highly unlikely. It may not even determine the career field you choose to follow.

Your first job need not make or break you. People change jobs and even careers many times in a lifetime, and probably so will you. "I never felt that if I hadn't gotten myself slotted into my career by twenty-five that it would be the end of the world for me," says Kathleen Conway, a supervisor of training services. "That kind of thinking is limiting; it's no good. I don't think you should have to feel that what you've decided at twenty-two is it—that it's your life."

Women in particular have often failed to develop a long-range approach to their careers. Although the Cinderella myth has changed somewhat, many women still suffer from the "Cinderella complex." "In the back of their heads," says Ms. Kraft, "they're still thinking, 'Well, I'm going to work for a few years, and then I'm going to get married and have children, and then I don't know if I'm going to work anymore.' I don't think young women have a clear idea of what they want to be in twenty years. Whereas a young man coming out of school will tell you much more readily what his long-range career plans are."

Getting Over the "Cinderella Complex"

For any "closet" Cinderellas who may be reading this, these statistics about women and work may help startle you to abandon the "Cinderella Complex":

- Women now make up 49 percent of the entire labor force.
- More than 50 percent of all working women are married; 48 percent have children.
- The number of married women who work increased from 40.5 percent in 1970 to 46.6 percent in 1977.
- Over 8.6 million women live alone (1973).

Even if you are waiting for the Prince (or if you have found him), the rising cost of living and ever-more-gloomy economic predictions make it highly unlikely that you'll be able to retire to your castle and live a life of luxury. And if you choose to remain single, it's likely that you'll have only yourself to depend on for your daily bread and butter. That's about as good a reason as any for making long-term career plans!

Women often suffer from an additional lack of foresight; they come into a first job thinking, "I'm going to do this job the best I can forever," instead of saying to themselves, "What skills can I learn here and where do I want to take them?" Your first job is an important beginning, but it is not an end in itself. It's a stepping stone to other jobs in your career.

One woman we interviewed stayed on her first job for nine years. "I was afraid of making changes," she told us. "The job was my family, the one constant in my life. I left it kicking and screaming!" Developing this type of "till death do us part" attitude about your first position (or any job) can only close out many other options for you.

What if you don't make the best decision in choosing a first job? That's not a death sentence either. If you think of your career as a pyramid of building blocks, the first job is the one in the center of the bottom row. From there you can go up or sideways. If your first job is less than ideal, you can build on what you've learned from the first "block." As Karen, a former first-jobber, told us, "I hated my first job and couldn't wait to get out of it. But I did the best I could to improve myself and learn new things because if there was another opportunity in the company, whatever I learned would be important." Remember, no matter how "good" or "bad" your first job is, you can walk away from it with some valuable knowledge—about your work, yourself, the work-world realities your education or life experiences never taught you.

Your first job is an opportunity to test your wings, to see if you can fly. Where you want to fly and how far up you want to go are things you'll have plenty of time to think about once you're airborne.

FROM SCHOOLWORK TO PAID WORK: MAKING THE TRANSITION

2

GETTING OUR FIRST professional position is an experience few of us will ever forget, both for the excitement it can produce and for the uncertainty and disillusionment that it can also bring. Making the transition from student to full-time worker can sometimes be more difficult than many anticipate.

Part of the problem is that first-jobbers often erect a one-way barrier between school and work. Once that barrier has been crossed, they think it's impossible for them to return to the other side. They tend to think of school as a place for learning and of work as . . . well, as a place for working. Somehow the two never seem to mesh. Graduation marks the end of their lives as students—now that they've put in their time as "learners," they're going to put all that acquired wisdom to good use.

As Lansing Lamont points out in his book *Campus Shock,* "We encourage our children to enter college as though it were at once a passport to maturity and an escalator to prestige, security, and a high income." With this type of attitude, it's no wonder that so many first-jobbers are disillusioned when they discover that they're not magically equipped to take the plunge and get right at it.

Nowadays that piece of paper otherwise known as a college degree is not a one-way ticket to fame and fortune. The truth is that at graduation, your education has only just begun.

"Listen and learn," advised one woman manager we interviewed. "The first year of starting out in your career should be a good learning experience if you keep your eyes and ears open. But if you come in with preconceptions of what your first year *should* be like, what you *should* be doing, how you *should* be rewarded after that year, you might be in for a disappointment. I came in very open-minded and really hoped to learn. I think with that kind of attitude you will succeed."

In addition to the barrier often erected between education and work, new graduates face yet another stumbling block. Many former students have not had a very accurate view of the business world. Many first-jobbers have had little or no previous work experience. Even in the case of those who have worked, the types of jobs traditionally held are not those that can give a broad overview of what the world of work is really like.

"One thing I found when I just got out of college was that I was a real greenhorn," recalls Jane Nemke, an employee relations administrator for the Weyerhaeuser Company in Wisconsin. "I was very naive about the ways of the business world, naive about what level you've got to reach before you're given authority to make decisions. I think it took me a good six months to learn the ropes."

Jane's experience is not atypical. "People coming out of school have an unrealistic view of the business world," says one recruiter we talked to. "They have an expectation that the business world is waiting for them to come in and create all these innovations and apply all the knowledge they've gained. And they do get into the organization, but it doesn't work the way they thought it would. So they become frustrated. They bounce around from one place to another. Eventually they find out that business is pretty much the same everywhere."

No One Told You It Would Be Like This. . . .

"Okay," you say. "So business is pretty much the same everywhere. But what does 'pretty much the same' mean—what is it like out there?"

"School ain't work" is how one first-jobber put it in a nutshell. And that's right on target. The very fundamental differences between the school and work environments take some getting used to. As John Shingleton and Robert Bao observe in their book *From College to Career:*

> The way our educational system operates may have conditioned students to expect similar experiences in real life. On the contrary, most of the rules governing academic life bear little resemblance to those operating outside. Such gaps may be called "systemic" since they result from differences inherent in two different systems with different goals.

These "systemic" differences can make the school-to-work transition more difficult. "What I found hard in making the transition," said Juana, a first-jobber, "was the idea that you can't take a vacation when you finish something big. In school you have exams, then a vacation, and then you go back and pour yourself into it again."

That is right: work is not on a semester system! There's no midwinter recess or three-month summer vacation, and that realization can come as quite a shock after you've been on the job for a "semester." "At first it seemed impossible that you wouldn't have free summers," said Carla, a management trainee. "When I first started work, I thought

I couldn't stay more than a year. I said to myself, 'How can anyone keep working without breaks, doing the same thing year after year, without any letup?'" People *do* work for an entire year with no semester breaks. It's something that first-jobbers have to adjust to.

Am I Flunking?

Living without semester breaks is just one of a first-jobber's necessary adjustments. Another common complaint we heard was that no one really tells first-jobbers how they're doing. In school, your work was evaluated very clearly and on a regular basis. You wrote a paper and got a grade; professors had office hours when they could tell you just what they thought of you and vice-versa. Basically, you knew pretty much where you stood; unless you were truly in trouble for some reason, you could usually avoid flunking before the end of the semester.

At work the situation is not quite the same. "You have to realize," says Susan Dresner, formerly a manager at McGraw-Hill Information Systems, "that you're not going to get grades. No one is going to pat you on the back regularly and say to you that you did well or you can do better; I find this is infrequently done in business. It's expected of you to do the job."

Unfortunately, many first-jobbers aren't prepared for the no-grade system. For one thing, grades have been so important to them for the past twelve or more years that they may find it difficult to operate without such definite feedback on their performance.

Karen, one first-jobber we talked to, had expected to get a lot more evaluation than she has received on the job. An editorial assistant for a small magazine, she was sure the "higher-ups" in the organization would want to give her a lot of "grades." "After all," she says, "they're putting their name on the product as well." But, she told us with some dismay, "Here you get not a kind word, not a pat on the back, nothing!"

If you're not getting any opinions about your work, it's often better to take matters into your own hands. "It always pays to ask how you're doing if you're not getting any feedback from a superior," says Jane Nemke of Weyerhaeuser. "I've found that I was always much better off asking rather than trying to guess, or waiting until someone volunteered the information."

If lack of feedback isn't hard enough for first-jobbers to handle, there's something else in the picture that often compounds the problem: when they do receive praise or criticism, they may not even know it. "A person on his or her first job," according to Steve Moresca, a financial writer for *Business International,* "won't really know how he/she is doing for the first six months or so. Unless of course, it's very obvious. For instance, if each time a person hands in an assignment their supervisor gives them a look of utter dismay, they will sense that they're not doing too well! You really have to get to know the people you work for and with—and you have to learn to read the signals they put out. Some people will actually be complimenting you, and you wouldn't know it because you haven't learned to 'read' them."

Who's in Charge Here?

Students' lives are externally regulated by the school environment itself. Professors give assignments, hand out lists that enumerate exactly which books to read for a given course, and sometimes, much to the delight and relief of many a student, even disseminate exam questions in advance. And on a few jobs the situation may be quite the same, for some supervisors suffer from latent "professorism": they prefer to tell their subordinates exactly what to do and when and how to do it. If you can then "play" the student, everything is fine. However, the majority of work situations are not as highly structured as that. Yes, you're expected to do the work, but precisely how and when you do it may often be your own responsibility to determine.

"Unfortunately," says Judith Warner of Consolidated Edison, "that's where the educational system really fails to prepare you. Everybody tells you what to do in school, reminding you seven times to bring in a paper. If you miss an exam, you're given twelve different make-up dates to choose from—the professor lays it all out for you. Nobody is going to do all that for you on the job, but a lot of recent graduates expect them to, wanting their supervisors to tell them exactly what to do every minute."

If you can take the initiative on the job yourself, you're a big step ahead. Unlike the situation at school, in the work world you must decide priorities for your own tasks, and often set your own deadlines. You can't blame bad grades on the professor anymore. If you don't deliver, it's your problem.

If you missed a class in school, it generally wasn't a big deal. You'd get the class notes or assignment from someone else. But "it's not the same if you miss a day of work," said one first-jobber. "You always have to pick up where you left off. Problems don't go away easily; and there's not always someone there willing to fill you in on the 'assignment.'"

"But I'm Not Going Anywhere!"

Many first-jobbers also suffer from the "semester syndrome." Students can usually count on being "promoted" at least twice a year—into the next semester. "Promotions" came regularly and at fixed intervals in school. At work, it's a different story. Promotions don't necessarily occur with any regularity, and sometimes they don't occur at all. This point may seem like a very obvious one, but the fact that students are used to rapid advancement can make their transitions to work harder. Since as students they become so conditioned to advancement at a fixed rate, many first-jobbers become impatient when they are required to remain in one job or at one task without a promotion for longer than a "semester." They begin to feel they're not moving anywhere, and as a result many leave their first jobs much too soon.

Many first-jobbers also come to the sudden—and sometimes too late—realization that their employers expect much more from them than just a passing grade. Although you'll hear those ubiquitous stories about so-and-so who's never done an honest day's work in his or her life but is still president of XYZ Company, the general rule is that marginal effort on the job only leads to mediocrity, or worse, to termination. Valued employees are the ones who are willing to give a little extra, and generally they're also the ones who get promoted.

One first-jobber comments on her all too real appreciation of this work-world fact of life: "It's a great emotional upheaval for someone just out of school, and to whom learning came as a matter of course—one who didn't really have to push for good grades—to discover that at work you really must 'sweat' to get ahead."

Obviously, not all employees make that extra effort. They fulfill only what's required of them and do an adequate job, period. How much "extra" you are willing to give is up to you. It's a choice that you can and will have to make—one that can lead to success or mediocrity on your first job.

A lot of adjustments must be made in changing from "student" to "worker." But everyone invariably makes them. It may take longer for some than for others. But, as you know, tadpoles turn into frogs, caterpillars turn into butterflies. Students become first-jobbers; first-jobbers, successful career women. You too will survive the metamorphosis. But by becoming aware of some of these very basic differences between the school and work environments, first-job employees *(and* employers) can take a big step toward making the transition easier for themselves and those around them.

"RETURNING" TO WORK? WHAT ARE YOU WORRIED ABOUT?

Many women who are making an initial entry into, or returning to the paid labor force after having been home for several years, have some uneasy feelings about their "first" jobs. What concerns you most?

- Do you feel you might not be able to meet the pressures of the working world?

- Are you unsure whether you would be able to fit in because of living so long in the style of mother or housewife?

- Are you worried about how you will be able to meet the work world's expectations?

- Are you fearful of losing some things that you value—for instance, friendships, community acclaim, or family praise—if you decrease some of your home-based activities?

- Are you unsure of your capacity to integrate being a wife-mother and a career woman?

- Are you afraid that a mother-substitute may not be good enough for the maternal care you want for your children?

- Are you worried about the effects on your husband of your earning level or rank in the work world?

- Do you feel uncertain of your husband's and children's willingness to help you and support you in the ways you will need?

- Do you feel that supervising men on the job would be inappropriate or too difficult?

- Are you fearful that your husband will be made unhappy by your independence?

- Are you afraid that your children or husband—or both—may feel deserted because they are used to having you at home?

Write down any other uneasy feelings you have—like the ones above that other women have had. Examine them and determine whether some of them can be relieved—either by getting some more facts, additional formal education, or some professional counseling, or by just "talking it out."

Begin now by rehearsing, in your mind, how you will handle any tacit or verbal criticism, disappointment, or anger of someone who feels neglected by your new schedule. Will your child's whine about your absence at lunch hour upset you, or will you be able to explain quietly that he and you will have time together at a later hour? Will your husband's annoyance over your absence from home on a day that he has off be a major problem, or will the two of you be able to work out a comfortable understanding of each other's individual needs and schedules?

These problems may be considerably minimized if you involve your family, at frequent intervals, in your thinking, exploring, assessing, and planning. Your local library or bookstore is likely to have some books that deal with the problems of returning to work. (See bibliography.) Reading one or more books or articles may be helpful, in part for the information they offer and in part for the reassurance they provide by telling of other women's experiences as they entered the work world after a period of absence.

There will be rough spots—times when people are impatient and don't understand at all, when everybody seems to want everything at once, when there are simultaneous crises at home and at work. Some days or weeks will flow by unrippled; others will be full of currents that push and pull. If, however, you keep your long-range goals in mind, and permit yourself to "sleep on it" at the end of some days of frustration and discouragement, you are very likely to find yourself with a career life that is rewarding in the ways you hoped for and planned.

3

THERE'S ALWAYS A FIRST TIME: SOME TRITE BUT TRUE WORDS OF WISDOM

"VERY FREQUENTLY," according to career counselor Barbara Holt, "a woman brings into the work situation the sense that she ought to be perfect or not make a mistake. Learning that to be mortal means that we are imperfect is a whole big experience!"

Yes, we are mortal (at least, most of us are); and, unlike the mythological Athena, most of us do not pop out of Zeus's head fully grown, equipped with an armor plate and the wisdom of the ages. But sometimes we think we do, in which case we suffer from what is called the "Athena complex."

"Women are obsessed with being perfectionists," says Susan Dresner, formerly of McGraw-Hill. "When they make mistakes, they personally and emotionally blame themselves. Women should have a sense of humor about themselves and their jobs—it will help them when they do make mistakes. My advice to first-jobbers is, don't take mistakes so seriously—all that is expected of you is to correct the mistake quickly and without too much fuss."

Mistakes: Getting Over the "Athena Complex"

For those of you who may be suffering from the "Athena complex," here's our Wise Saying #1: *Don't be afraid of making a mistake.* At first, you'll have a certain "grace period" when you will still be learning the ropes and are expected to trip up every now and then. This doesn't mean that mistakes are totally unimportant and that you shouldn't care when you make one. And it doesn't mean that you shouldn't always demand the best from yourself. What it does mean is that no one does everything right the first time out; face the fact that you won't either.

Barbara, an apprentice plumber in a company research plant, learned her lesson the hard way. "Last week I made my first 'big' mistake. We'd been putting up some piping and it turns out that I didn't tighten something sufficiently. When we turned on the faucet, there was this huge explosion of water. We all got drenched and I got *very* embarrassed. But no one was upset at me. They said, 'Look, you're going to make mistakes, it's all a part of training. Don't worry too much about it.' I can guarantee I won't make *that* mistake again!"

And we got the following story from a first-jobber, a staff writer for a large magazine: "We always get calls from the press in our office. Whenever a reporter is working on a story and needs some background information on a topic we're very knowledgeable about, they'll give us a call. We're supposed to pass all these calls to our senior editor. Well, one day we got a call that I thought was really unimportant and didn't feel warranted the editor's attention. So I just gave the reporter some basic background information; he took my name and the name of our magazine. Little did I know that his article was going to be syndicated and that I would be quoted in thirty newspapers around the country! We rarely get clippings from reporters but it just so happened that this reporter sent me about fifteen clippings from the story! I was so proud of myself; I showed a copy to the senior editor. Well—she really blew her stack! She said that I didn't say the right things, and that I was quoted out of context. She went on and on. Although I thought her reaction was totally exaggerated since I still felt that the story was really unimportant, I was *very* embarrassed. But I learned that from then on I should pass on *all* press calls to her—no matter how trivial they seemed to me."

Needless to say, this writer survived her mistake and is none the worse for wear. (She has since gotten a promotion and a salary increase.) When you make an inevitable (and forgivable) mistake, the most important thing to do is to figure out why you made it and how you can avoid it next time. And admit your mistakes honestly and openly, for there's nothing worse than a person who tries to blame his/her error on someone else. It wouldn't do you any good to ignore a mistake, and if you implicate someone else, it might jeopardize that person's job.

Oscar Wilde once wrote that "experience is the name everyone gives to his mistakes." We all have a "How-could-I-have-done-such-a-stupid-thing?" story. But making mistakes is a part of gaining experience. For every mistake you make, you should learn something new. Besides, cheer up, for each time you're wrong, you'll probably have been right at least five times—the odds are in your favor!

Patience Is a Virtue . . .

"To those who are plunging headlong into the business jungle with their BA or MA mortarboard and tassel still attached," said first-jobber Nina, "I would particularly stress the importance of maintaining an attitude of patience. I am continually amused by the job-advice columns in magazines that scream: 'Always be ready to jockey for positions!' Certainly, after one has been on the job awhile and has learned the ropes, this advice is sound. But in the beginning, don't expect too much too soon."

Wise Saying #2: *Patience is a virtue you will have to cultivate.* There are no rags-to-riches stories in the real-life work world; no one becomes president overnight. It takes time. Expecting instant success on your first job will only lead to instant disillusionment. People and things frequently don't proceed as quickly or as efficiently as most of us would prefer.

Patience will help you in other respects also. As a new (and largely inexperienced) employee, you will be expected to prove yourself—after all, no one really knows yet what you can do. Part of proving yourself involves paying your dues. Since you are the "new" person, you will invariably get stuck doing tasks you consider trivial and not worthy of your immense talent. Some work tasks no one likes to do; they must be done anyway. But it is a difficult lesson to learn. One administrator recalled how frustrating it was for her: "In college I had always been a straight A student; I had always been at the top of my class. Then I got my first job and I was at the bottom of the totem pole doing really boring things. All those wonderful college courses where you have all kinds of decision-making exercises and challenging case studies to do aren't anything like the real world and your first job. And it *was* disillusioning. I thought, 'Why in the world did I get a master's degree when I could've gone to third grade and do what I'm doing?'"

Whatever you want to call it—grunt work, drudge work, junk work—part of learning any new job *is* what more experienced employees may think of as junk work. Learn the discipline of doing things you don't necessarily like on your first job. It will be a valuable lesson: you can't expect to love every single work task you will ever perform. But take the bad with the good. It's a part of the job.

Don't make the mistake of thinking that junk work doesn't pay off. "When I first started," says Carol, a first-jobber, "I expected to do all the drudge work—and that's what I got. But I found that in doing drudge work you get a quicker view of everything. It has its rewards. You learn the processes involved, you're in on the bottom, and you get an overview of how everything works."

Barbara Seymour, an audit manager for a large department store, agrees. "It can be a real drag in the beginning. There's a lot of clerical work that leaves you wondering, 'Why did I go to college for this?' But you have to look at it as an investment. If you don't learn the nitty-gritty yourself, how can you supervise anyone else?"

Unquestionably, drudge work is hardly the most inspiring endeavor you can undertake. It can lead to some psychological traps for first-jobbers. Sometimes they get bored too easily because they expect everything to be a peak experience. "It never occurred to me that I'd have drudge work to do," says Linda, a young woman on her first job as a marketing assistant. "Filing, filling out messenger slips—all that stuff. But I've learned to accept that it's part of any job. In the beginning I felt as if I had to do something substantial *all* the time; I needed a sense of contributing something worthwhile every day. I'd feel guilty if I had to devote a day to catching up on correspondence or administrative tasks. And I almost made the mistake of ignoring it and getting so disorganized that I could have lost my job. Sometimes I even wanted to quit, I felt so bored. But now I realize that the seemingly piddling stuff is just as important as the fun, exciting work—it's what makes it possible."

Knowing that everyone else does his share of junk work will not necessarily make it any easier for you to bear it. And junk work never really goes away—you may get concentrated doses of it at first until you've proven yourself, but twenty years from now, you'll probably still have tasks that you *hate* and that have "drudge" labeled all over them

However, there are ways to get drudge work done with a little less pain. (Some helpful hints appear in Part III.)

What if I Can't Handle It?

Just because you've spent the better part of your life in school, that doesn't mean that you're an unqualified person with no obvious talents. But many new workers succumb to that feeling. "When I first started working," recalled first-jobber Mike, "I thought the whole world was smarter than I was."

This feeling is a natural one because as a first-jobber you're really not sure yet of what you can do. Your potential is largely untapped. You might feel confident in the sense that you're bright, you received good grades in school, you got your degree—those are things you can be sure of. Whether you'll know how to write an effective memo, conduct yourself at a meeting, or even convey to others your competence are matters you have no tangible proof of as yet.

Wise Saying #3: *Don't underestimate yourself, for you probably know more than you think you do.* One primary requirement of any job is plain old common sense. And most of what you will need to know for your first job can be picked up quickly. Having the confidence you need and being alert and ready to try something new is half the battle.

Self-confidence comes with time and experience. "In the beginning I felt very inadequate," said Marcy. "But as I've done more things at work, I've gained a lot of self-confidence. I no longer feel as if I have nothing to contribute."

We are all unsure in the beginning; but that first success—when you've done something well and you can say, "I can really do it"—will go a long way toward dissolving much of your initial insecurity.

Good, Bad, and Indifferent

Our fourth and last Wise Saying: *It's not going to be easy; but who said it would be?* Yes, we admit it. There will be times when you'll be tempted to run out and apply to the nearest graduate school. There will be times when everything seems to be going wrong and you can barely write your name, never mind pull together a report for the boss. And yes, there will be times when it seems that every human being has been put on this earth with the express purpose of making your life miserable.

Kathy McCoy, a freelance writer living in California, likes to tell the following story to women just starting out. As a former editor at *Teen Magazine,* she was required to go out and interview a *very* conservative businessman. Unknown to Kathy, she was also suffering from pneumonia at the time. During the interview she collapsed in a dead faint. When she woke up, her head was on one of her interviewee's shoes.

Needless to say, Kathy was embarrassed. Whether they'll admit it or not, everyone in your company has had one of those "I-was-so-embarrassed-I-could-have-died" moments. But we all have our success stories also. By sharing other people's experiences, blunders, and triumphs (you *will* triumph), you can develop a sense of perspective about your own situation.

We asked Barbara Holt, career counselor and owner of an executive search and recruitment firm, for some words of wisdom for the uninitiated:

In our career counseling workshops, we talk about the fact that if we ever had to do anything as difficult as that which we do in the first twelve to eighteen months of our lives, we'd spend the rest of our years in bed! For instance, since we've presumably all accomplished it, we talk about a child learning to walk. The very first thing is that the child knows that she is going to do it. She hasn't read any books on how to walk, there's no pro-walking movement, and there's no legislation about walking—she doesn't even have an intellectual concept of mobility. She simply knows she's going to do it. That knowledge is the first thing one has to have. Long before we decide what *it* is, we have to know we're going to do it.

The second thing that happens is that you or I stood up and we tried our first step and—we *landed!* And we tried again and—we landed. And again, and again. Each one of those falls represented pure and simple failure; we tried to do something and failed. But the point when we indeed would have failed was if we decided we weren't going to get up again. That's the second thing that's necessary—the recognition that failure is not simply an external judgment, but a bit of a choice, an option. And we can do something about it.

The third thing that the child does is to ask to be picked up, perhaps, or go back to crawling for a while, or whatever. But she looks for nurturing; we unlearn that as we grow older. We learn that it's selfish, or it's wrong. We tell ourselves: "Stop thinking about yourself!" But I suggest that it's probably essential because there's no other way to revitalize yourself.

So, know you're going to do it, deal properly with the fact of failure, and—take care of yourself!

4

READY, WILLING . . . AND NERVOUS: FINDING YOUR NICHE AT WORK

> You can't eat for eight hours a day, nor drink for eight hours a day, nor make love for eight hours a day—all you can do for eight hours is work.
>
> WILLIAM FAULKNER

NO MATTER WHAT anyone tells you, it's not always fun being a new employee. You sometimes feel that everyone in your new office is staring at you, until you begin to wonder if you've sprouted an extra head. You don't really know the company, and you don't *know* your job yet. So you may tend to feel a bit out of it—especially since everyone else seems to know exactly what's going on. Even worse, you've noticed the easy camaraderie shared by your new colleagues in the office. At first you may feel very left out—as if you hadn't a friend in the world!

This brief but overwhelming period is when most new employees begin to feel very sorry for themselves and wish fervently that they were back in school. Being the "new kid in town" is something *everyone* goes through, and is something you'll go through more than once—assuming that you'll have more than one new job. The best that can be said for this period of orientation/awkwardness is that it won't last very long—a few weeks at most. In the meantime you'll be too busy to feel sorry for yourself for very long.

And remember, although you may be feeling a bit insecure at first, whoever hired you obviously had confidence in your ability to do the job. If you don't *feel* very smart, at least you must *look* and *act* smart. And that's a step in the right direction.

It's important that you use these orientation weeks to your best advantage. It's the best time you'll ever have to sit back, listen, and *observe*. As first-jobber Nancy put it: "At first all you should bring to your job is your warm body and your *attention*. Lending your own color to what you do comes later." Just think of yourself as a very big sponge—start soaking everything in!

You should aim for three things during this period: to get to know your job, to get to know your company, and to get to know your colleagues.

Learning on the Job

The main weakness of most orientation programs is that they do not tell the new employees what they need to know to get started doing their jobs. What is told is often a tremendous amount of confusing information concerning retirement, insurance, stock plans, time sheets, company organization, and other items that might be better left to another time and another method of presentation.

Training and Development Journal,
January 1979

Most likely you've heard that employers like employees that are self-starters, right? Well, they do, but you should be given some sense of direction in the beginning, or at least a little shove to get you going. The amount of actual training you will or won't receive depends largely on the size and nature of your particular employing firm. Generally speaking, the smaller the company, the less "formal" the training you'll receive. Employers such as banks, insurance companies, retail firms, and other large corporations often have very structured training programs. These programs can last for any period from a few weeks to a year or more. Some rotate a trainee through several departments over a given period of time, and some combine classroom work with supervised on-the-job or field experience.

Programs such as the latter can often give you that "back to school" feeling. As Diane, a trainee at a life insurance company says, "I almost feel like I've only gone from one semester to another. Every night I go home and have homework to do! It doesn't feel like I've progressed very far."

For other first-jobbers, it's the reverse situation. "This company didn't offer *any* formal training sessions," recalled Doreen, an internal auditor. "It was pretty much do-it-yourself on-the-job training . . . kind of scary. You had to recall everything you could theoretically from your textbooks, apply a lot of common sense, and hope that you just got through it."

Patricia Foster, a copywriter for a large retail store, had a similar experience. The training she received was also very informal: "It consisted of going around and looking at the merchandise on the second floor, which is the gallery floor, and also on another floor, where children's clothes were displayed, and seeing what it looked like and talking to the buyers and some of the salespeople, and then figuring out a way to sell those particular items which were going to be advertised—in a very forceful way." Her first presentation was accepted, but her second was not. In this way, over a period of months, Ms. Foster was "trained" in the specific format that the store wanted—to write to certain specifications—and gradually she gained credibility in her capacity to broaden her base in the area of copywriting.

Other employees, however, prefer informal training. Mary Hogikyan of Potlach Industries in San Francisco is one. On her first job with a legal firm, she was thrown right into the thick of things: "You didn't feel so much like a student," she recalls. "You felt that you were actually working. I think it was better that way because it forces you to pick yourself up and learn the job and do it; no one had time to pamper you."

Whether your early training is formal or informal, it's important that you put your best into learning the job you're being paid to do. If you're learning new procedures, pay careful attention and take notes. Ask questions! Don't be afraid of being a pest. It's much better to ask than to muddle through and then discover that you've done something all wrong.

Observe the skills required to do your job and evaluate your own competence and needs in view of these requirements. If you find that you don't have much background in a certain area, take the initiative and try to fill it in on your own. "You should present yourself as being eager to learn," advised advertising executive Marilyn Arato. "Instead of doing just a specific task, try to learn all aspects, expose yourself to other things and their relation to you."

And remember—all the success strategies in the world won't help if you don't master the basics first. Don't ask for big new challenges until you've met the small new ones. Putting the cart before the horse has never worked—the cart just usually falls over!

Whom or What Are You Working For?

Getting to know your company means a lot more than finding out who's president and where the nearest coffee machine is. It means learning a company's rules—both the written and the unwritten ones. It also means really learning about the business of the business—what the company's purpose is and how it achieves its ends. Why take the trouble of learning so much about your new employer? Because the interest you take in your company will probably be reflected by the interest they take in *you.* Besides, it helps you do a better job when you know how, where, and why all your blood, sweat, and tears are being spent.

All companies have rules; some may be clearly stated on paper—the company's personnel policies, for instance. (You'll probably get some kind of brochure or booklet when you are hired. Read it carefully.) Companies usually have some not-so-obvious rules also. For example, just when *do* you have to get in for work?

The emphasis placed on punctuality is one of these "unwritten" rules. Some employers expect you to be right on the dot—with reason. Your presence or absence may affect someone else's ability to proceed with his or her job. Other companies may be more flexible, and you'll just be expected to be "responsible" about it. Fine. But in the beginning, it's better to play it safe and be on time—even if the only person you impress is the elevator operator.

At first you may show up bright and early and rarin' to go at 8:00 A.M., only to discover that you're the only one there. "I used to really sweat to get into the office right on time," said first-jobber Carol. "But then no one else did. At first I thought everyone just wasted a lot of time. What with getting coffee, and the usual morning bantering, work doesn't usually begin till 9:45. But then I quickly realized that no one was leaving at 5 either. So the company gets its money's worth."

Other unwritten rules may include the length of lunch hours (Is it really an hour?), or even how you dress or decorate your work area (more on those later). You'll discover these rules pretty quickly as long as you keep your eyes and ears open.

During this period, take the initiative to learn as much

as you can about your company's business. "I would hope that a woman coming into a first job would immediately begin to investigate just what her company is about," said one employee supervisor, "where it is going and whether it is going to be a good vehicle for her career development. What are the names, who are the people; what are the central functions, what are the peripheral functions; how important is your department and how does it fit into the rest of the organization? By asking yourself these questions you can begin to get a clearer picture of just where you and your organization are heading."

"To get ahead on your job," advises Kathleen Conway, "be interested in everything that goes on. The most annoying thing to supervisors is if someone is in a little box and just does the work that comes across the desk."

Copywriter Patricia Foster concurs. "You don't just sit there and do what they tell you to do. That you are absolutely functioning all the time you're there, all eight or nine or whatever hours you spend working, is understood; but you also are expected to learn the functions of other departments—not just yours. That way you will begin to see how they interrelate and how the company operates as a whole."

It's not necessary to play private detective in order to get the "lowdown" on your company. You will learn much, of course, from your new boss and colleagues. Other valuable sources of information include annual reports, profit statements, publicity files, press releases, and in-house newsletters and magazines.

This advice seems all too obvious, right? Wrong. As one first-jobber pointed out, "You'd be surprised how many people sit at their desks from nine to five oblivious of what's going on around them!"

"Listen, look, and smell is what I suggest for the first job," says manager Susan Dresner. "Keep your eyes open and take the bull by the horns. This doesn't mean you should come on like gangbusters—that's nothing but obnoxious. Follow office hierarchy; learn and stand on office ceremony. Respect and acknowledge people's titles."

What else should you be learning? A lot. For instance, study your new benefits. Clear up any questions you may have concerning vacations, personal days, leaves of absence, life or health insurance plans, medical services, continuing education programs, and any other fringe benefits your company may provide. If there is any office equipment you may have to use and are unfamiliar with, learn to operate it as soon as possible. Find out where the office supplies are stashed or what procedures to take to get what you need. The sooner you learn these things, the faster you'll become accustomed to your new job.

First-Timer in an Old-Timers' Club

At times I still feel self-conscious about being so young. At first I really felt like an oddity. I thought everyone must've been wondering, "Who's that kid?"

By the time you're a senior in college, you're beginning to feel very "old" and mature. Suddenly, in the working world, you're treated almost like a baby. It's like being a freshman all over again.

FIRST-JOBBERS

You'll be spending forty or more hours with your coworkers every week, so how you feel about them and how they feel about you is very important. Getting to know your new colleagues will take a lot of time and energy during your first weeks on the job.

If you haven't already done so, on your first day of work you should ask your new boss or supervisor to give you a little guided tour and introduce you to your new colleagues. It might be a good idea to take along a pad and pencil to jot down the names of the people you meet, their functions, and locations. (If you work in a very large office, a list like this can be invaluable.)

In general, the best advice we can give is to let relationships with your coworkers develop naturally and gradually. Believe it or not, all those names will turn into real people, with real problems, likes, dislikes, and individual personalities. Be careful of stereotyping your colleagues on the basis of first impressions, which can often be misleading. As one first-jobber told us, "It's hard to reverse an opinion once it's formed."

You will of course come to like some of your coworkers more than others. And while you may ultimately have a good working relationship with everyone at the office, there'll probably be one or two colleagues that you really call friends. But don't align yourself too closely with any one person or group immediately. "You have to be wary," says Michael Kraft, "because new employees are often prone to being befriended by an individual who may not be the best person to be associated with—someone who's negative or on the outs with everyone else. So they'll latch on to the first new person that comes along." Be cordial to everyone, but adopt a "wait and see" attitude at first.

And don't worry if you're not getting lunch invitations on your first day there, or that you aren't being included in after-hours socializing immediately. Your coworkers will also probably be a little reserved until they get to know *you* better. You must give them time to warm up to you and vice-versa.

Some first-jobbers, anxious to be accepted by the new "crowd," overcompensate and act overly friendly and cooperative. This behavior can work against you in two ways. First, it may be misconstrued as insincere or overweening flattery. "The first-jobber who comes in the first day saying, 'I'm new here, let's have lunch so I can find out what you do,'" says one woman manager, "well, that can really put people's teeth on edge. They'll wonder, 'Who is this spy?' You have to be careful of coming on too strong."

Trying too hard can work against you in other ways. It can lead a few not-so-nice people to take advantage of your friendliness. "I was so anxious to please one of my new supervisors," recalled Martha, "that pretty soon I was doing errands for her at lunch and even picking up her dry cleaning. It wasn't long before I realized that she was really exploiting me, and I stopped it before it got out of hand."

"Aiming to please is okay," says Susan, another first-timer, "provided that you're not running out every two and a half hours for the office coffee-fix. Don't overextend yourself on such things—it's counterproductive."

How's Your Space?

No, we're not talking TM, or EST, or even Zen. We're talking about your work area. As a novice to the work world, one thing is certain, you won't have much choice as far as your office space is concerned. As a beginner, you'll be issued your little piece of the turf, ranging from a desk amidst a sea of them to a partitioned cubicle to, if you're lucky, your very own, very small office. In other jobs you may even be out on the field most of the time in a lumberyard, manufacturing plant, or other nonoffice setting.

Whatever you get, what you do with that space should be in keeping with your position and with the tone of the company. Don't rush into decorating. Take a little time to get acquainted with your new environment and find out how your other colleagues have managed.

It's natural that you'll want to personalize your work area and place your stamp on it. However, decorating the office is not the time to use all those handy-dandy tips you've gathered from the pages of *House and Garden* over the years. Your work area is not the place to dump all the excess knickknacks that don't fit anywhere at home. And unless you work at a recording studio, it is not the place to put your very favorite poster of Bjorn Borg either.

Use your own common sense when it comes to "doing up" your space. Obviously if you work in a very conservative bank, what you can or can't do will be very different from your choice if you work for a flamboyant ad agency. Often companies might have stated policies with regard to office decor—perhaps for fire prevention, safety, or esthetic reasons. "There are certain walls we can't touch around here," said one first-jobber. "It's written down as company policy." Usually, however, how you personalize your work space will be left to your discretion. "We just know we can't do anything drastic," said another young woman. "You just have to look around and sort of come to your own definition of what 'drastic' means."

Cutting out your favorite "Doonesbury" cartoon and pasting it on your wall may be fine if you work at a local lumberyard, but your friend at the corporate headquarters might tell you it's a no go over there. Definitions of "drastic" will vary considerably.

Still, it's important that you have a few things of your own that please your eye as well as your mind. You'll probably be spending eight or more hours in your space, five days a week; so you're entitled to a few personal touches—if only for the sake of maintaining your sanity!

For those of you blessed with a green thumb, plants can add a nice touch to your work environment. One woman who has a small corner of her office full of beautiful, well tended plants has received more than one compliment for her little garden. However, be wary of overdoing it. If your hair gets tangled in your Boston fern, and the Venus's-flytrap is beginning to crawl into your *In* box, you may have gone a bit too far. (And if you have a reputation for killing off every plant you've ever known, don't keep any in your office. There's nothing sadder than a poor little brown plant wilting in a corner. Besides, it will make you vulnerable to accusations of cruelty to living things.)

As a matter of convenience, you should keep a few necessary thigs either on, in, or near your desk. These can include the following (but adapt our list for your own situation):

A wall or desk calendar
An agenda for writing your daily schedule
Some pads for writing "to do" lists or informal notes
An index of phone numbers and addresses
A good lamp or light
A good dictionary
Some pens and pencils that *work*
A few safety pins
Tissues
A bottle of aspirin (You'll need it, believe us!)

If you are the supercareful type, you could also consider keeping an extra umbrella, a pair of stockings, some makeup, and a hairbrush stashed away somewhere. (But be careful of turning your work space into the closet you don't have at home.)

On the subject of neatness vs. messiness: Remember Felix and Oscar on the old *Odd Couple* television show? One was fastidiously neat, the other equally messy. Well, the work world is full of Felixes (Felicias) and Oscars (Oscarinas?). The Felixes are the ones that have a single pile of papers centered right in the middle of their desks; their files are in order, their *In* box is neat—in a word, their work areas are pristine. The Oscars, however, thrive on clutter. The more stacks of papers, books, files, the happier and more productive they are. (Then there are those few hardy souls in between who feel obliged to clean out their desk at the end of the week, or at least shove everything into an empty drawer.)

Again, the degree of messiness or neatness you can get away with will vary from employer to employer. In some companies a cluttered office might be the "home" of a "creative" mind; in other places, however, a cluttered office is taken as a sign of a cluttered mind—no good.

Take a look at your colleagues' offices (particularly the higher-ranking ones). If you find that they all seem to be competing for the Tidy Homemaker Award, you may have to suppress some of your Oscar tendencies and literally clean up your act. It's also a good idea to emulate the style of your boss. At any rate, if your messiness (or compulsive neatness) starts interfering with your work, you'll have to change. (Some tips to help you appear in Part IV.)

Another caveat about your office space: As a first-jobber, you're more than likely to be sharing office space with one or more colleagues. Aside from the very obvious lack of privacy, sharing space can cause some other difficulties.

"I found it really awful at first," said first-jobber Claire. "We had over twenty people in one large room; we each had a desk and a piece of the wall, and basically that was it. Sharing close quarters means that if you're looking for distraction, you could easily find it. It was a simple thing to just turn around and start talking to someone. If there was a loud discussion going on, you'd have to join or leave the area because there was no way to ignore it. You had nowhere to hide or to retreat to."

What can you do in such situations? Nothing much unless your employer decides to partition off the area. You have to try and muster up all the powers of concentration at your disposal, ask for everyone's cooperation, and do your job. After all, that's why you're there.

From Blue Jeans to . . .

Thoreau (remember him from Lit. 101?) once wrote: "Beware of all enterprises that require new clothes." Well, that sentiment is fine if you've chosen a career as a hermit, but the chances are you will need some new clothes for your first job. If you're like most recent graduates, you've probably spent a good deal of your life in denim. You know, you had your shabby, broken-in jeans for school, and then there was that "dressy" pair—the nonfaded ones—that you reserved for special occasions. Life was very easy. Unfortunately, not even your "dressy" jeans will get you very far with most employers, and on your new job you'll be expected to dress the part.

Just as with your office decor, your office clothing should be in keeping with your position and the tone of your company. Again, analyze your employer and see what the rest of the office is wearing. This doesn't mean that you have to turn into a clone and wear exactly the same outfit that all the "successful" women in your company wear. Just as you would want to personalize your office space, you want your clothes to say something about you. But remember that at work you will not only be projecting your personal image but will also be reflecting the company's image. The basic question you must ask yourself is: "Is my clothing appropriate for *this* work situation?" For instance, if you work on a construction site, you'd probably wear overalls to work; if you worked in the fashion industry, you'd probably be expected to look trendy.

"It really depends on where you're working," says Jane Nemke, who works for Weyerhaeuser in Wisconsin. "When I worked at my first job in another company, how I dressed said whether I was a secretary or part of management. Here it's a different situation. The forest-products industry tends to be very casual. The vice president comes in with blue jeans and cowboy boots; dress is just not a part of management. In fact, if you do dress up, everyone wonders what other job you're interviewing for!" Follow your company style and work demands.

As a general rule, it's best to keep your work clothes neat, simple, and comfortable. In the beginning especially, and until you've gotten to know your work environment better, dress conservatively. If you find that you spend the entire day pulling down your hemline, pulling up your neckline, and untangling the three chains you're wearing around your neck, you may have overdone it.

If you really need some help deciding on your work image, many books have been written on how the upwardly mobile career woman should dress. (See Suggested Reading.) When we asked our interviewees about the usefulness of such books, we received varying responses:

"I couldn't believe what one of those authors was saying," said one woman manager. "I think dressing is personal style; I *hate* anyone telling me what to wear. In our office, we don't have a stated policy as far as dress is concerned. We just understand that it has to be conservative. You've got to use your common sense and dress according to the environment. I think people who read those books and follow them to the letter are really insecure about themselves."

Other women, however, found these books helpful. "Dressing is very, very important," said one personnel executive, "and you can pick up some valuable information from those books. When I see women at work dressed in a very cutesy or flashy way, I don't know if I want to be associated in business with them. I don't want to be lumped together in the 'Look at the dress she has on today,' and 'Boy, is she coming on strong' categories. You have to be careful with the way you dress. *Very.*"

Now that you're aware of the perils and pitfalls of on-the-job dressing, how can you build up a suitable work wardrobe? The first thing to do is to stand in front of your closet and cast a critical eye on everything. Next, put all the denim things into one pile. Separate anything that's left into "suitable" and "not suitable" piles. ("Suitable" of course means appropriate for work.) Analyze what you have. Is there a basic color scheme? What can you mix and match? For instance, if you have one black skirt, you can wear it with three blouses for three separate looks. Is there anything that belongs in the Goodwill pile? Be ruthless. If you're not going to wear something, eliminate it. It will only take up space.

Next, sit down and make a list of new clothing you think you will need. It's a good idea to decide what clothing is really essential, because the chances are that you won't be making enough money to spend on a whole new wardrobe. For instance, two good investments would be a suit for winter and one for summer in some basic colors. Suits are appropriate for practically any occasion, and you can adjust their look by changing tops or wearing them with or without the jacket.

When you do forage into the department store jungle (or wherever you do your shopping), keep a few things in mind. If you limit your choices to some basic, contrasting, or combining colors, you'll get a lot more mileage out of what you buy because you'll be able to mix and match different pieces of clothing. Beware of buying very faddish things. Fads have a way of disappearing rather quickly and then you're stuck with an expensive "something" that you may never wear again. Also, if you hate ironing and can't afford dry cleaning, keep these points in mind as you select clothing of different fabrics.

Finally, buy what you think is best for *you.* If you're going to feel or look uncomfortable with a particular article of clothing, it's not going to help your image. Some good advice was offered by Ted Scott, a vice-president at a large bank: "My conviction is that effectiveness comes from being who you are. It takes some doing to be aware of yourself and how you feel and look best. I tend to be a militant individualist, and I say to both men and women: 'Dress and look the way *you* think is most effective in order to accomplish the things you want to do.'"

(And cheer up—even if you do hate the kind of clothes required for work, think about how good it'll be to slip into your nice shabby dungarees when you get home!)

Part II
On the Job

INTRODUCTION

WHETHER YOU REALIZED IT or not, you were not only hired to get things done, you also were hired to get along with people. There are times when your *magna cum laude* status or your 100-words-per-minute typing speed or your special talent in a particular area won't count for much. Granted, you had to show some native intelligence and skill to get your foot in the employment door. But the determining factor—the real reason you were chosen from among all the other sparkling candidates who clutched résumés similar to yours—was most likely because your employer felt you'd *get along*. On the job you are required to get along with—work well with—the boss, your colleagues, the folks in the mail room, the person who pushes the coffee cart—any and every breathing soul in the company. Getting along, you see, is a great deal of what work is all about.

You may have never thought of success in the work world in terms of getting along. You never were handed any rewards in grammar school for attempting to relate to Johnny, the class troublemaker. Sure, it might have put you in good stead with your teacher, but as far as upping your grades from B's to A's—no chance! So to help you get a good idea of what the work world is like, think of it as a second chance to get along with all the Johnnys you neglected in your school days. And imagine you're getting graded for getting along: D, you're fired; C, you're holding onto your job by the skin of your teeth; B, the job is yours for life; A, you've been promoted one rung up the ladder— to deal with the next batch of Johnnys.

Stop thinking of your job solely in terms of the work involved. But do pay close attention to your boss and coworkers. Especially if you have a glimmer of success floating in your head. Your ability to deal with people will largely determine your success on this, your first job, and on all the other jobs in your career path.

5

THE BOSS

REMEMBER LEARNING IN SCHOOL that stereotypes are wrong, and that we should judge each person we meet on his or her own merits? Then why is it one of the few stereotypes we still cling to is the boss stereotype?

Even if you've never worked a day in your life, you have developed some assumptions about what a boss is like. And the report card is not good—you probably have come to believe that a boss is cold, insensitive, unfair, authoritarian, unreasonable, mean, cruel, and nasty. In that order.

Part of this unfavorable picture stems from what we've seen and heard on television and in the movies. (Who can ever forget Lucille Ball's tyrant of a boss, Mr. Mooney?) But a good deal of this boss stereotype probably came to us from our parents. How many times did your mother or father come home from work, grumbling about the boss— "that blankety-blank-blank"? (Expletives deleted.) With such negative influences, it wasn't possible to grow up truly open-minded about bosses.

All Shapes and Sizes: Debunking Boss Stereotypes

Still, you'll be better off if you can cast that stereotype aside before you start working. To help in that effort, ask your friends and relatives about their bosses. You'll probably hear they're really not monsters after all, but for the most part they're talented, humane, considerate people who possess a few idiosyncrasies. They're just like the rest of us. And do give your boss the benefit of the doubt. After all, he or she is probably giving you it too. ("She's not lazy like the rest of her generation. She won't run away with her Prince Charming after only six months on the job.")

Don't underestimate the importance of that first working relationship with a boss. Your first boss is the person who introduces you to the world of work, and those first impressions tend to stay with you for your lifetime. Although you'll be the last to admit it, you'll probably adopt some of the beliefs and behavior of your boss, just as you took on your parents' while growing up. Put simply (we can't stress this point too much), your first boss will be a key figure in your life. So get your relationship with that very important person off to a good start.

What to Expect from a Boss

Now that you're willing to rid yourself of the negative boss stereotype, how about also changing your thinking about what subordinates can expect (remember, you're one of them). The chances are that you're still in proud possession of an "appease thy boss and sacrifice thyself" frame of mind. Well, it's time to shake it: the boss-subordinate relationship is a two-way street. Of course you'll be expected to do many things for your boss, but he or she is also expected to do some things for you to make your on-the-job experience as worthwhile as possible. The eight following rules for bosses detail some of the things you should be able to expect from a boss.

#1: *Your boss should train you.* He or she should give you a sense of direction. Your boss should provide you with feedback on your performance, letting you know how you're progressing, what your strong points are, what you still have to develop. And as you master each new assignment, he or she should provide you with new ones. According to Susan Moskowitz, manager of training services at New York Life Insurance, "A boss should put you on different projects so you can be given the opportunity to prove yourself in a variety of situations." You should be permitted to go, for example, from accounts payable to accounts receivable, or from one part of the production process to another. In short, it means your boss should see to it that you grow on the job.

#2: *Your boss should get to know you.* You should begin to feel that he or she has a sense of who you really are, and what your needs and wants are. You should feel that your boss's door is always open for you to go in and discuss problems you're having.

#3: *Your boss should set high standards for you.* He or she should demand the best performance, for that's the only way you'll really learn. As Barbara Alwinson, a civil service employee, recalled, "My first supervisor was like your old English teacher type, so picayune you wouldn't believe it! But even though she was difficult to work for, I really learned a lot about setting standards for yourself." One boss we heard about refused to read any activity reports or memos that her subordinates handed to her that had typos or glaring grammatical errors. She'd make them rewrite and retype those reports till she was satisfied. Her staff would curse her under their breaths as they furiously typed away, but once she accepted the reports, they felt proud that they had measured up to her standards.

#4: *Your boss should act as a buffer between you and*

others. In effect, your boss should take on a big brother or big sister role, acting as your intermediary with people in other departments and between you and his or her boss. If there are any skirmishes to be fought, your boss should do the fighting. If you need any information that you've been unable to get from others, your boss should retrieve it for you.

#5: *Your boss should blow your horn for you.* Your boss has a direct pipeline to his or her boss, and often, the upper echelon of the company. If you've done a particularly good job, your boss should let the people who count know about it. This service is just part of your boss's taking an active interest in your career, and seeing that you get on the right track to a promotion. As Louise Brannon, a campaign manager of a statewide campaign, says, "A good boss is one who lets his or her people get the credit for their own work. That's particularly important for women. You can't go around to anybody looking for a job and say, 'I wrote this report' if it doesn't have your name on it. They'll just say, 'Oh, yeah?' I've been lucky. My bosses have let me take credit for what I've done well, and I've done the same thing with people working for me. It's a credit to a boss to develop good people."

#6: *Your boss should keep you informed about your company.* If the board of directors will lose three members, he or she should let you know and tell you how it will affect your department. Don't expect your boss to tell you "all" all the time, however. There will be information he or she will have to keep privy. But the important information— like the fact that your entire division may be eliminated!— should come first from your boss, before your friend Tom in the personnel department breaks the news to you. And even though your boss would hate to lose you, he or she should keep you informed as to all openings in the firm as they occur.

#7: *Your boss should give you some freedom in your*

work. Many bosses are so concerned that their subordinates' performances are a reflection on them that they constantly look over their workers' shoulders, insuring that they never err. If you've been told to check with him or her before making every decision, you know you have such a boss. Bill Murray, a management development specialist with a major retail company, had this problem with one of his bosses: "I had to get permission to do everything. In consulting work, you often have to make a decision on the spot. I couldn't. I had to go back and check it out. That was embarrassing, because around a client you want to feel like you're a person with some importance who can make his own decisions." A good boss should give you just the amount of latitude you need, and be willing to let you make mistakes and learn from them.

#8: *Your boss should try to be open-minded.* A boss must listen to what the subordinates have to say and allow them to disagree. Ginger, a legal assistant, said her boss admitted to being a "benevolent despot." "She'd let you have your say," says Ginger, "but listened with a deaf ear. She always wound up doing things her way. After a while everyone stopped arguing. 'Why bother, it won't change anything,' we all said." Ginger's boss was not open-minded. An open-minded boss is someone who really listens to what you say, and is able to admit that his or her way is not always the best way of doing things if that truly is the case.

You've just read what in essence can be considered a description of the perfect boss. We've yet to hear of one boss who practices all the above all the time. (If yours does, you're not working for a mere mortal, but a saint. Check to see where his or her halo and wings are hidden.) As long as your boss makes a stab at most of the eight "rules," you're in pretty good hands. But if he or she has yet to practice one, don't interpret it as a sign that your boss is out to make life miserable for you. Your real problem might be that you have an uninformed boss. So do a little educating. We don't recommend that you photocopy the preceding pages and leave them on your boss's desk! But we do prescribe some frank and open communication. It's your responsibility to tell your boss how he or she can help you do your job better and be a happier employee. As with most relationships, a good way to make your life with your boss better is to be both understanding and persistent. It may take work, but your reward will be a key ingredient to success in any job.

What Your Boss Expects from You

In this mutually beneficial relationship of yours, what can *you* do for your boss? Basically, there are two things you can do: One, make your boss look good in the eyes of others (remember, he or she is out to climb that corporate ladder just like you—the higher you can help hoist your boss, the higher you'll go too); two, try to make life easy for him or her (your boss has a boss to answer to also). You may be asking, how can I do these things, and carry my work load as well? The answer: Consider this effort part of your work load. It's an essential part of getting ahead. The following four rules will help you both make your boss look good and make life easier for him or her.

#1: *Find out what tasks your boss dreads doing,* then ask to take them on or at least help out with them. If you keep your eyes open, you may notice that your boss hates handling customer complaints, or would sooner lick envelopes than write up an expense account. Then go to your boss and state that you'd be more than happy to assume those duties, if it's all right with him or her. *Always ask first.* If you barge ahead without asking, your boss might feel that you're muscling in on his or her "turf," that you're after his or her job. Bosses can sometimes be sensitive in that way, as you would be in that position. So tread carefully.

#2: *Let your boss know when he or she has made a mistake.* This rule requires a lot of diplomacy and tact. Say you've spotted an error in a presentation your boss is supposed to deliver to the president of the company. Maybe she or he's been giving you a hard time of late and you'd like to have your revenge (ah, sweet revenge!) by letting the mistake be noticed by the president. But if you ignore it and keep your mouth closed, you'll only hurt yourself in the end. Your boss's status reflects on your own. If she or he's made to look like a fool, people will assume that you must be a fool too. It's called guilt by association. So be loyal and be on the guard to help your boss do well.

#3: *Cover for your boss.* If your boss's boss calls at 9:30 and your boss isn't in yet, don't say "(S)he's not here yet!" But don't lie either. Say, "(S)he's not at her desk. Can I take a message?" Or better yet, "Can I help you with anything?" But if your boss is habitually late because he/she knows you'll cover for him/her, and it's making you uncomfortable, then do have a talk with your boss. Perhaps your boss is being unfair and exploiting you. Good communication usually will avoid such problems. Cover for your boss, by all means, but also know when to draw the line.

#4: *Be loyal to your boss.* Don't gossip about him or her to others in the office. Loyalty means being a friend too. Your boss will have bad days when your support will be needed. Listen to his or her problems; offer your understanding and help. The higher you go in a company the less feedback you get from anyone. So your boss will appreciate hearing how she or he is doing from you—if it's presented to help, not hinder. And when your boss deserves to be patted on the back for a job well done, do it. You'll find that he or she will do the same for you one day.

When You and Your Boss Disagree

It's inevitable. No matter how well you get along with your boss, there'll be times when you just don't see eye to eye. Conflicts are to be expected and even encouraged. If you didn't fight now and then, you're probably hiding things from each other, or as the saying goes, sweeping a lot of dust under the carpet. So get it out. Talk. Learn to put aside the feelings you have for your boss and deal solely with the issue at hand. If you're angry, it's not really your boss at whom you're angry. It's his or her behavior. Learn to distinguish between the two.

And above all, fight fair. Turn to your boss when the problem first starts to surface, not after it's been going on for months. Jesse, who worked for the production supervisor of a manufacturing firm, didn't know how to "fight fair." Her boss had been dumping a lot of personal duties on her for about five months. Finally Jesse decided to have a showdown over the matter. She marched into the supervisor's office, sat down, and calmly began to state her grievance. Her boss, who had been standing motionless, looking out a window with her back turned toward Jesse when she entered the room, remained in that position all through Jesse's diatribe. This behavior angered Jesse so, she suddenly burst out crying, "I hate you, I hate you!" Well, Jesse's boss stood her up and escorted her back to her desk. Before leaving her there, she made a point of telling Jesse's coworkers that they should be especially nice to Jesse, because after all, "She's just not herself today."

Needless to say, Jesse's boss was partly responsible for provoking her outburst. But part of the blame lies with Jesse herself. She had not gone into her boss's office to discuss her problem until she was really boiling and much too distraught to deal well with the matter.

When you have a conflict with your boss, don't think of it in terms of a legal case. Don't wait week after week to pile up incriminating evidence. Actually, you don't ever want to sound accusatory. What you do want is to let your boss know your feelings about a particular situation. And the best time to do this is when you're slightly grieved, not all worked up to a fever pitch—because when you're at the boiling point, your boss might react to you as Jesse's did: "You're not yourself today." So go to your boss when the problem is still in its early stages and your emotions are still under control.

Another point to keep in mind is that you should handle the conflict in private, not before an audience. Pat, Gina, and Dorothy share desks in a travel agency with their boss Lillian. Privacy for them is a hard commodity to come by. So when Pat wanted to discuss a problem with Lillian, she waited till Gina was out to lunch, and then asked Dorothy to run an errand. Pat did the right thing. It serves no purpose to discuss a touchy issue in front of your colleagues. Actually it's unfair to them—they'll feel embarrassed and uncomfortable if they have to sit through your session with your boss. Also, don't feel you must give your coworkers a blow-by-blow of what went on between you and your boss. It's your private business; keep it that way.

Once you have your boss's undivided attention, start by stating the problem as you see it. Describe your feelings. If you think you know your boss's motives for his or her actions, mention them. Have a solution ready that will be acceptable to the two of you. Evelyn had gotten annoyed by her boss's new practice of writing memos every Monday, detailing her assignments for the week. Evelyn felt this showed little respect for her intelligence and abilities. This is what she said to her boss: "I'm deeply troubled by the memos you hand me every Monday. I know you're aiming for greater productivity from me, a goal I appreciate. But these memos leave me feeling very insulted; I can figure out my assignments for the week without being told. Actually, I'd much rather inform you, either in writing or by just telling you, what I feel I should be doing that week. This way I know I'll be learning more." Notice how Evelyn figured out her boss's reasons for writing the memos; how she spoke honestly of her feelings, but not in a way that was accusatory ("these memos make me feel insulted," not *you're* insulting me"); and how she came up with an answer to the problem that in all likelihood her boss could accept. That's what fighting fair is all about.

Another warning you may not have figured out for yourself: Never *ever* go over your boss's head on an issue. It doesn't matter how important it may be. You may be under the impression that your boss's boss will lend an impartial ear to your gripe and mete out justice. Wrong. Your boss's boss doesn't have an impartial ear. He or she is more interested in supporting your boss and maintaining the hierarchy than in playing King Solomon. Well, you say, *your* boss's boss is different. Maybe he or she is. Maybe you will get the justice you're after. But consider the ramifications—how will you ever be able to reestablish your working relationship with your boss if he or she knows full well you can overstep him or her again? Be prepared to live with the consequences if you disregard this caveat. Better still, take our warning to heart.

Look at each conflict that arises as a learning experience. The higher you go, the more people you'll have to deal with, the more conflicts you'll find yourself in. Learning to handle conflicts is an interpersonal skill you must acquire somewhere along the line. It might as well be here and now, on your first job.

When the Chemistry Isn't Right: Working for Someone You Don't Like

After the job interviews with you, your boss probably came away with a pretty good feeling that the two of you would get along just fine. And you probably left the interviews optimistic yourself. In case you've already forgotten, "Gee, I really liked her. I think we'll work together well" were your sentiments at the time.

But, to borrow a song title from *Porgy and Bess,* "It

Ain't Necessarily So." During the first few months the two of you may carry on like bosom buddies. Then, when that "good grace" period ends, the two of you reveal your true personalities, which may happen to clash like a mighty pair of cymbals. You're outgoing; she's an introvert. You're very detail-minded; she's sloppy in comparison. She prefers to beat around the bush; you like to be told things straightforwardly. Your friends begin to tease you, calling you two "The Odd Couple." You're hard pressed to find any humor in the situation and are ready to throw in the towel.

Before you do, think about what's at stake. The first job is the one in which you learn the most about your field. And if your boss (yes, the person you don't like) is the one teaching you, it's best to hang in there until you've learned everything you can from him or her. All it requires is changing your attitude. Try, if you can, to separate your job from your boss. Jennifer, a woman on her first job, found this tactic helpful. She worked in a clothing store run by a very temperamental woman who was constantly snapping at her. Jennifer walked around that store always on the verge of tears. But she held onto the job. "I respected my boss's knowledge of retailing," Jennifer says. "I knew I had a lot to learn from her, even though I didn't like the woman."

While you're sticking it out, as Jennifer did, keep any resentment you may be feeling toward your boss inside you. Don't badmouth him or her to others. Remember: your boss is probably not the only one in the company evaluating your performance. You wouldn't want any noticeable hostility toward your boss ("I absolutely hate him!") to stand in your way.

And don't hide from your boss. One young woman resorted to calling her boss on the phone whenever she had a question to ask her so she wouldn't have to go into her office. She even avoided going to the same women's room— for fear of running into her. Her example is not one to follow. Always maintain a rapport with your boss. Up until the day you leave—and even thereafter—you'll need your boss's cooperation and trust. You'll never win them by hiding under your desk all day.

Learning to work with someone you don't like is what being professional is all about. If you consider yourself professional, you had better act like it.

When Work Styles Clash

We all have different work styles, different ways of approaching and tackling our work. Going into your first job, you may think that it will take a while before you develop your own style. But the chances are that you've had one all along. In school, did you start a term paper two weeks before it was due, or did you attack it the night before? If you were the night owl, it's still likely you follow this "day before" regimen. Your professors may never have gotten wind of your work habits, but now that you're employed, they're noticed by everyone—especially your boss. And it may be that your boss is not a proponent of the "put everything off till the last minute" philosophy of life. If so, you're in trouble. It's very likely that the anxiety your boss suffers over your dillydallying (as he or she calls it) may soon be passed on to you.

A more classic case of clashing work styles involves the "clean desk" boss and the subordinate who hasn't spotted the top of her desk in months. "A sloppy desk indicates a sloppy mind," he may tell her. "Neatness is a sign of mediocrity," she may have the gall to return. Kathy McCoy, a former Features Editor for *Teen Magazine,* admits quite proudly to having kept a messy desk. "My desk and office were such a sight that my coworkers made me close my door when the fire department came for an inspection. But I didn't mind the mess—I worked quite well on mounds of paper. Anyway, it was my own personal statement."

Granted, we all need our own personal statements; they help us maintain our sense of individuality in what can be a very conformist environment. But what do we do when our statements are not the kind our bosses want to hear? As Margaret Hennig and Anne Jardim stated in *The Managerial Woman,* women are too fiercely loyal to doing things their own way: "Women's responses, centering on . . . who one is, place much less weight on others' demands and expectations: 'This is who I am—like it or leave it.'"

Most career consultants agree with Hennig and Jardim in that "like it or leave it" is not the stand you should take when work styles are involved. They recommend that you watch your boss closely till you get a good sense of his or her work style, then imitate part or all of it. It may be how she organizes her work load, or the way he handles a problem, or even the way she keeps her desk. In other words, if he wants a report started one week before it's due, get going; if she keeps a neat desk, do thou likewise (though the reverse—your piling up a mountain of paper to match your boss's desk—doesn't hold true, you'll be relieved to find out).

The justification for these copycat antics is to keep your boss happy, and to score points with him or her in the process. Your boss will notice that you're emulating his behavior, and this to him will seem the sincerest form of flattery.

As for yourself, don't look on what you're doing as "selling out" to corporate conformity. Rather, think of it as part of the process of getting where you want to go.

"I Can't Get Any Support Around Here!"

At the very least, you should expect support from your boss. That means your boss's standing by decisions he or she has made, you've made, or the two of you have made together.

Let's say your boss told you to hold up on sending a brochure to the production department until you can double-check the sales figures going into it. As a result, you've been deluged with hysterical calls from the head of production. You may think you're the one who should be calming that person's ruffled feathers. You're not. Your boss is the one. And even if your boss has never spelled out how you should handle such a situation, don't feel awkward about referring the production head to your boss—politely, of course.

You see, although you may have always felt you can "look after yourself," at work, your boss is in a much better position to do that. Let your boss fight the battles; people will listen to him or her. Face it—in the scheme of the business world your boss has more clout, authority, power (call it what you may) than you. There'll be a lot more victories chalked up on your and your boss's side if you let him or her do the sparring.

What if you have a boss who's handed you his pair of boxing gloves? All those disgruntled souls you calmly referred to your boss have now been sent right back to you? Even if you don't mind handling that sort of thing, you should still inform your boss that you feel you don't carry enough weight to deal with the office malcontents. Tell your boss that position means something to those people: "They'll listen to you, not me." And try to come up with a solution that may make your boss's dealings with the office folk easier. Maybe he doesn't care for one-on-one confrontations. Then suggest he use the phone or correspond via memos. And perhaps there's a way your boss could avoid boxing matches altogether. One way: if he'd inform people ahead of time of his decisions. If the head of production had received a memo two weeks earlier that the brochure might be a couple of days late, that department's deadlines could have been changed accordingly. Then there would have been no need for the ranting and raving that did take place. You must offer support in order to expect support back.

Support also takes the form of your boss's promoting an idea of yours to whomever it is you need to convince or impress. As manager Bill Murray points out, "You're seldom allowed to advocate your ideas all the way up. At some point, someone takes an idea over for you and takes it up higher." That "someone" is usually your boss. But do make sure that your boss is passing off the idea as *yours,* not his or her own. If you're attending a meeting with your boss, and your boss presents your idea "as a thought I've been playing with for the longest time," refrain from butting in with a "Hey, wait a minute—that's my idea!" Talk to your boss after the meeting. You may find that your boss had a legitimate reason for having "stolen" your idea. For instance, presenting that idea as her own may be just what she needed to recapture the favor of her boss. Thus her "stealing" your idea may do more for the two of you in the long run. But if you see this practice turning into a habit, it may signal other things. Perhaps your boss fears giving you the recognition you deserve, thinking she'll lose you then. Or by making you look too good, she may feel that everyone (most of all her boss) thinks she's not doing her job. At that juncture, though, regardless of her motive, it's time for you to take action.

Get credit for your ideas by putting them in black and white. Write memos and pass them to your coworkers, your boss, his or her boss, and any other important superior. (Also, slip a copy into that all-important career file you should be keeping for when résumé-updating time rolls around.) Even if the situation does change and your boss starts giving credit where credit is due, keep churning out those memos. They're a sign that you're proud of your work and are committed to getting ahead. In all likelihood, they may help you get there.

Dedication vs. Exploitation

When was the last time you turned to a friend and said, "Boy, is my boss ever exploiting me! If I were getting paid for all the hours I put in and the amount of work I do, I'd be making three times more than I am!" If these words sound too familiar to you, you'll be pleased to know you have a lot of company—there are hundreds of women out there on their first jobs who, like you, are hurling charges of exploitation at their bosses right and left.

Are you all justified in your complaints? Is it a fact that people on their first jobs are more prone to being victimized by their bosses? No. The problem is that you and your boss have your signals crossed. What you perceive to be clear-cut signs of exploitation—long hours, no overtime pay, little verbal gratitude—your boss considers requisites of your job. You see, your boss expects you to act like him or her, like a professional. And professionals aren't clock-watchers, nor do they expect to be thanked for that extra effort. It's part of their job, and also, they hope, of yours.

But, you say, *he's* the one making the professional salary, holding the fancy title, and occupying the glamorous office. *He* can afford to act like a professional. But what do *I* get out of acting like a professional? It's a fair question. Unless you can see the pot of gold at the end, what's the point of following the rainbow?

If, for instance, you one day want to have a managerial position like your boss's, you can see the validity of acting professional now. It will be your way of showing your boss how serious you are, how committed to getting ahead. But what if you're unsure just what you want to do, or whether this is the type of company for you? You can't see the point of being so dedicated because you may not be around for very long. In the meantime, your boss is pressuring you to stay late and to take work home. Why doesn't he understand?

Bosses, it turns out, work under the assumption that you're satisfied with your job and want to grow in the company and one day even have their job. Very few are able to recollect the uncertainties they felt when they first started working. Susan Moskowitz, a supervisor of training services, is one of the lucky few who can remember: "Sometimes I look at the workers here and think they're doing what's required of them, but they're not giving it that extra push. But when I think back in my career, when I started working, I did my job and did it well. But did I put in that much extra? No. That's something that came a little later, when I saw a place for myself."

If you're feeling as if your boss doesn't understand your point of view concerning "that extra effort," maybe you should sit down with him or her and have a good, long talk concerning your true feelings about the job. Don't worry. You won't get fired if you tell your boss you haven't yet found a place for yourself at the company, or if, in fact, there may not be a place for you. As Celia, a former accounting trainee, said: "I always thought accounting was for me. But after a year I realized it wasn't the kind of work I'd see myself staying with. In the meantime my boss was badgering me to work on weekends, attend special conventions with her, the whole bit. She really wanted to see me advance. I thought it was only fair to be honest with her. So I told her. She was disappointed. But from that day on to the day I left, she no longer insisted I work late or do extra traveling. It really helped to clear things up."

Be sure also that you're not the one who's doing the exploiting. Roberta is quick to admit that she and her boss get along like good friends. "Before I knew it, I was taking advantage of his good will. I'd come in a little late on Monday, take a two-hour lunch on Wednesday, leave early on Friday. I realized I was doing those things because he wouldn't mind. Well, he should have minded. I was using him, and all in the name of friendship."

And if you ever come across a boss—male or female—who befriends *you* to excess, be somewhat wary. That friendly relationship may turn exploitive.

Take Sarah's case. Sarah works for a one-woman public relations firm and says she liked her boss from the start: "Dorothy insisted we work like a team. She never wanted to be a lordly boss but wanted to treat me as an equal, not a subordinate." All was fine and good until Sarah found out that by being Dorothy's equal, she was expected to play the role of "surrogate psychiatrist." Every day she had to listen to Dorothy pour out her heart about her marital and financial problems. "I really feel she's taking advantage of me," says Sarah. "I don't want to hear about her personal problems—I don't have any answers for her."

Don't look to your boss to be your soul mate. He or she can't be, and it's unfair for either of you to be put into that role. Leave a little distance between you. It's healthier that way—you both know where you stand.

QUEEN BEE OR KINDRED SPIRIT: WORKING FOR A WOMAN

With women entering and reentering the job force at a phenomenal rate (we now constitute 49 percent of the labor force), and with increased efforts to advance women into managerial slots, it is very likely that at some point in your career path you'll be working for a woman.

What will she be like? How should you act toward her? Again, you'll do yourself a lot of good to get rid of all those damaging stereotypes. There's the one Joan Crawford helped immortalize—that of the woman boss as shrew. Or the stereotype that is nothing more than an updated Crawford—that of the woman boss as antifeminist, or "queen bee." ("She had to kick and claw her way to the top and will expect you to do the same.")

But the latest stereotype to hit our midst is perhaps the most unfair, though on the surface it seems the kindest of all. That is, woman boss as sister, kindred spirit, best friend. This stereotype was born in the women's movement, and is being nurtured in the ongoing drive to "humanize" the business world. The tenets of the "woman boss as soul mate" credo are as follows: she will accept and understand all your professional problems (she's had them all herself); she will accept and understand your personal problems and work around them (she's been there as well); she will treat you as her equal (she feels uncomfortable with authority).

The reason this stereotype is so unfair is that it places an unnecessary pressure on the woman boss. There she is, at last, where she wants to be, proud of her position, proud of being acknowledged as a professional. And there you are, expecting her to undermine herself professionally by granting you favored treatment because you are a woman. As one woman boss told us, "I have never been a sweet-talking or manipulative person. My philosophy has always been to treat people equally. I've never treated anybody in a special way because of their sex. I think the most important prerequisite of being a boss—male or female—is just to do the job well. If you establish your credibility and professionalism, both your staff and superiors will respect you."

Being a professional doesn't necessitate a person's acting in a cold and authoritarian way. There's plenty of room in the office for good nature, understanding, friendliness, and sympathy. But let your boss set the tone. Let her determine the way she'll act toward you. Don't walk in expecting her to treat you any differently from the way a male boss would.

YOUR COLLEAGUES 6

THE TRUE TEST OF your abilities to get along with people
comes when you work with colleagues. In dealing with your
boss, the situation was crystal-clear—you both had much to
gain from working together. If you helped your boss do his
or her job, your boss in turn could help you get promoted.
But what is there to be gained from getting along with
coworkers Don and Mindy, you say? You don't even like
them, so why should you make an effort to get along?

Look a little closer. Coworkers *can* help you succeed.
Work is different from school. Back then, you would
research a paper on eighteenth-century poetry yourself, or
study for a final with no help from others. When you got
your A, you knew you had done it all on your own. But
that's because you had all the pieces of the puzzle in front of
you. The nature of the work world, however, is such that
you may have two or three pieces, Jack has another two
pieces, and Millie has four. And you need those pieces.
Therefore you must cultivate a relationship with Jack and
Millie that will insure their cooperation and collaboration.
As Aurora Rubin, a manager at a major accounting firm
based on the East Coast, says: "You've got to like working
with people. You're hardly ever in the position where you
do a job yourself."

It's a Team Effort: Working with a Group

What Aurora is referring to is the concept of teamwork. That is, working hand in hand with others for the good of the whole. And in case you've been hiding under a rock for the last few years (and if you've been tucked away in academia, it may have seemed that way), the prevailing opinion on this matter is that women are poor team players. It all seems to stem from our childhood experiences. While we were playing one-on-one games like jacks, the boys were out playing team sports like football. And as Hennig and Jardim pointed out in *The Managerial Woman,* we always played with people we liked—our friends. This conditioning, they say, is responsible for our current problems with working on teams, which boils down to: "If I don't like so-and-so, why should I work with them?"

Well, you can take this theory however you please. There are women out there who work wonderfully in groups, though the only "game" they ever played in their lives was house. Then there are Little League boys all grown up who refuse to cooperate in business team situations. Maybe this woman-as-poor-team-players explains your on-the-job difficulties. Maybe it doesn't. What is important to take away from this theory is that you should be prepared to deal with people you may not like.

You may not be aware of it, but you've already had some practice in dealing with different and difficult personalities, with people you didn't choose to be with—your family. Remember how you used to wish your sister Fran was still but a gleam in your mother's eyes? Well, you may be wishing your coworker Evan never existed either. But if you managed to get along with Fran all these years, the chances are that you and Evan can work out a pact of peaceful coexistence too.

Actually, the family is a good analogy for you and your

colleagues. When you think about it, you'll be spending more time per week with the people at work than with your actual family. So during the hours of nine to five (or six or seven some days) your boss and colleagues will become, for you, a substitute family. And you'll be looking to get some of the same sort of emotional rewards from them that you get from your own family—a sense of belonging, of being liked, of safety. So it's imperative that you treat the members of your surrogate family well, with the same respect and esteem that you'd like to be given in return.

Conflicts and Confrontations

Conflicts will arise between you and your coworkers. You can count on it the same way you see that the weather seems to confront you with clear, sunny skies Monday to Friday, and showers all weekend. These conflicts have many causes. It may be that since you neglected to invite Janet to a project meeting, she's now charging you with dirty politics. Or perhaps you and Allen are ready to lynch Edward for never doing his fair share of the monthly reports you must compile, yet sounding off as if he does. Some conflicts arise out of simple misunderstandings that can be easily cleared up (you honestly weren't aware that Janet should have been in on that meeting). Other conflicts are more serious. They may stem from deliberate moves by your coworkers against you. If Gwen is stalling with the projections you need to complete your assignment, she may want you to be late, so you'll look bad. While you're temporarily in disgrace, she'll use the opportunity to look good.

Conflicts with colleagues can pose a problem for you, if you let them. Of course, you can always ask your boss to intercede in your behalf when and if things get particularly difficult. But it's your job to see that they don't get to that point. Try to reconcile your differences when you're still at the skirmish stage, not when you're in the midst of a full-fledged battle.

The most difficult thing to learn about solving conflicts is how to argue without flying off the handle. It'll take time before you're able to suppress all that anger you feel inside. Debra, a woman on her first job, said the first time she heard one coworker arguing unemotionally with another, she nearly burst out laughing. "There was Patty, screaming her lungs out. Hildy sat there, cool and composed, letting Patty rave like a madwoman. Finally, Hildy turned to Patty and without even raising her voice a decibel said, 'Patty, I can see you're angry.'"

Well, maybe you also view Hildy's behavior as comic. You may even feel it's unhealthy—Hildy, you say, will probably one day suffer from hypertension as a result of all that suppressed emotion. But realize that Hildy's calm, collected approach to arguing will get you further in dealing with coworkers than Patty's ranting. "Letting it all hang out" has yet to find its place in the work world. "Playing it cool" (and for "cool," read "unemotional") will always work to your advantage.

How do you "play it cool"? Good question. Let's create a confrontation for you. Say you've been having problems with Sally. You go into her office to talk, first depositing all your anger and resentment at her doorstep. You tell her that you feel this tension between the two of you that you'd like to clear up somehow. She refuses to talk about it. You try drawing her out, by asking a question: "Sally, what do you think is wrong between us?" Sally, you see, still directing on the inside all her anger and resentment *toward* you, needs some means of venting her emotions. Answering your question gives her a chance to release her steam. She explores: "Well, if you must know, you're always barking orders at me: 'Sally, I expect to have those notes by Friday.' Never do I hear a 'please' or a 'thank you' from you. You're

not my boss, Nancy. I don't have to be treated that way."
(Well, you did get what you were after—her viewpoint of
the situation.) Gracefully, you make your exit: "Thanks for
telling me, Sally. I think it can help matters greatly."
Remember: no counterattacks, no apologies.

Congratulations, you passed the one-on-one confrontation with flying colors—you were as cool as a cucumber!
Now, all you need to do to begin reconciling your differences with Sally is first to mull over what she's told you.
Give her words some thought. Maybe you have been curt
with her after all. Use a little kindness the next time you
have a request of her. On the other hand, you may have
been as sweet as molasses, and her contention that you've
been "barking at her" is unfounded. Then the thing to do is
try to put yourself in her shoes. She's already given you
some indication of what life is like from where she sits
("You're not my boss, Nancy!"). She just may be over-
worked and feel that everyone—including you—is dumping
on her. So the next time you deal with Sally, let *her* know
you know what she's going through: "Gee Sally, I know
you're answering to four people on this staff, and I can
imagine how hectic that must be. But I'd really appreciate
your completing these time sheets for me as soon as
possible." Empathizing with someone's plight can go a long
way. In all likelihood you'll probably see a marked improvement in your dealings with Sally. *Voilá*—the conflict between you two has ended.

Not every conflict with a coworker can be so readily
resolved. You may have tried to see things from his side and
changed any behavior of yours that irritated him, but have
been still met with resistance. If you feel you've done all
you can to get along with an intransigent colleague, then it's
time to go to your boss with the situation.

Office Friendships

War veterans have always said that unless you were down there in the trenches, you really can't understand what it was like. This same principle holds true for work. No matter how sympathetic your friend Terry is to all you tell her about that "absolute zoo," your office, she just doesn't react the same way as when you talk to Meg, your friend at work.

Having a friend in the office to share your grief and offer commiseration is important. But do be careful. There will be times when you'll find yourself having to criticize your friend's work, or compete with her for an opening. How your friendship will weather your getting promoted depends on how the two of you perceive your relationship. The office friendships that have worked out best are those in which the friends had an understanding, be it verbal or unspoken, that while on company time their loyalties would lie with the work at hand, and their friendship would come second.

Jackie and Paula have such an understanding. Jackie recalls that "there was this day when we were arguing over changing a sentence in a production report. Well, we discussed it back and forth until we decided to leave the sentence as it was. I felt angry over the issue and somewhat mad at Paula. But that didn't stop the two of us from going out to eat that evening, as we always do on Wednesday nights."

If you can't manage the sort of friendship Jackie and Paula have, then you'll either have to make huge sacrifices in your on-the-job performance to accommodate your friendship or end your friendship altogether. Think about it.

Competition

Competition is one fact of working life you've heard about—in books, movies, TV shows, and such—all about getting ahead of the next guy. So you've started your job and figure that the best way to compete is to outshine the competition. You get to work early in the morning, industriously attack your *In* box, diligently complete all assignments, ask your boss for more, work through lunch, and then present three brilliant (you think) ways of increasing office productivity at an afternoon meeting! You're pleased as Punch with your performance and feel it will get you far. But why is it that none of your coworkers have as much as said "hello" to you since you've started? Why the cold shoulder?

Well, you've gone about it the wrong way. Competing is one thing; being downright obnoxious is another. No one likes a whiz kid, especially one who's new on the job. A woman manager at a leading corporation explains: "You're just like the new kid on the block. People tend to resent you—they don't know where you're coming from." If they see you coming on like a house on fire, they'll resent you even further. Don't come on so strong at first. Take this advice from (Ms.) Michael Kraft of New York Life Insurance to heart: "When you start, keep your eyes and ears open. Keep a low profile until you figure out what's going on in that organization. If you come on too strong, you'll sometimes put people's noses out of joint, and everyone becomes suspicious of you. It'll then take a long time for you to overcome what you've done."

Laura, who's on her first job as a reporter on a newspaper in Indiana, agrees: "I wouldn't say I was 'mousy,' but my first few months here I listened to what other people would tell me even if I thought I disagreed with them. You've got to learn what's going on before you deliver your opinion on it. Some people become over-anxious when they start a job—they become pushy. If you lay low at first, when you do open your mouth everyone will *really* listen and you'll have the advantage of being much better informed."

And tread carefully at meetings, where you are on display and have a golden opportunity to sparkle—but also to incur the wrath of your colleagues. Some more advice from another woman manager: "Even though you're very 'gung-ho' and want to express yourself at meetings and say what you think is right, don't. People who have been there awhile will resent you. If you just kind of sit and watch at first—unless required to speak—it's better. After you've listened and been silent you can always open up. After you've opened up, your chance to keep silent and listen is over!"

Most people entering the work world view competition as a "kill or be killed" situation. But it's really not like that at all. There's more than enough room for everyone. Remember those *National Geographic* photos of all forms of wildlife calmly sipping water side by side in a jungle pond? Well, the work world is like that. You need not feel as if you have to knock off a few lions and giraffes before you find your place in the pond. There already is a place for you.

7

COPING WITH
OCCUPATIONAL HAZARDS

Is THERE A PERSON in this world who can honestly say that he or she doesn't mind receiving criticism? Probably not. We all like to think that we've made the right choices, that our judgments are impeccable, our tastes superb. Criticism tells us otherwise. And no matter if it's your mother giving you "her honest opinion" on the designer dress you bought ("It makes you look broad around the hips, dear") or your boss assessing a sales call you made ("You should have gone for the kill while you had him!"), criticism is hard to take.

But when you think about it, criticism, by its very nature, is not meant to make you feel good. That's the job of praise and flattery. But when they're not in sight, and criticism is knocking on your office door, or cubicle window, what do you do? You don't run. You stand there and take it . . . like a professional.

The Critical Point—Handling Criticism

First of all, learn to separate yourself from whatever it is you're being criticized about. Criticism is not an attack on your worth or competence or your very being. In the words of one first-jobber: "In accepting criticism, I have to make a separation between what I do and who I am." Nobody can ever touch the "who I am" part of you. Remember that. Simply regard on-the-job criticism as one person's efforts to help you improve your performance and your career potential.

Don't become defensive. If you're busy forming counterattacks in your head, you won't really be able to listen to what's being said. Judith Warner, a training administrator for a large utility company, says that when criticized you should be asking yourself, "'Where did I go wrong? What is the truth in this criticism?' Even if the criticism is wrong in many aspects, you can usually find some kernel of truth in it."

Ask questions. It's important to know what your strengths are and what you need to develop. In order for you to get a sense of what you need to clinch an important sale, or prepare a well designed layout, just ask. One line guaranteed to get you that information is: "What do you suggest I do the next time?" And although your boss or colleague may, as part of his or her criticism, tell you how you can improve your performance, you have asked first. Thus your critic knows that you're receptive and will follow his or her advice.

It takes quite a while to get used to handling criticism. As Carol Campbell, a woman on her first job as staff writer at a women's magazine, says: "The first time my work was criticized, I was on the verge of tears. Now, two years later, I still have problems. When my boss is sitting there editing my copy, I feel I have to leave the room. I guess I'm not hard-boiled yet."

Practically no one gets "hard-boiled" when it comes to dealing with criticism. Be prepared for a lot of it, especially on your first job. Why? In many cases the first job is largely a learning experience. Your boss and colleagues will probably go out of their way to teach you, help you, guide you—

in short, to criticize you a great deal. But it pays to listen to what they have to say. For the higher you go, the less criticism you'll receive, the less indication you'll have as to how you're doing. And that, in a way, can be more unsettling than being told.

Before you know it, the shoe will be on the other foot, and you'll be the one offering criticism. Maybe when you get promoted, you'll have to train the person who'll assume your old position. And a good part of training is extending criticism. How do you go about it? The wrong way is to come on like gang-busters, trying to reduce your "victim" to Jell-O as retaliation for all the times you were criticized. On the other extreme, don't come off sounding so wishy-washy that the person you're criticizing doesn't even realize that you are offering criticism.

Be firm and straightforward. Word your remarks so they comment on the work or performance, not the person: "Eleanor, your report lacked three important summaries," *not* "Eleanor, you weren't as thorough as you could have been in assembling this report." Leave it up to Eleanor to figure out why she left out those summaries.

It never hurts to add a little praise along with your criticism. Mary Poppins was right when she proclaimed that "a spoonful of sugar helps the medicine go down." Find something about the person's work to praise: "Eleanor, these recommendations for improvement you included in your report are well thought out and sound." Conclude your criticism by offering a suggestion for improvement—in other words, make your criticism constructive. "Eleanor, I find it very helpful when I'm doing a report to gather all the pieces together before I start writing. That way I can see right off if everything is there. This tactic may work for you too."

Coping with Postcollege Syndrome

Those first few months at your new job were exciting. Your colleagues were treating you like a real person, you were gaining confidence, learning new skills, and meeting a variety of people.

Lately, though, you've noticed that the novelty is wearing off a bit. Work isn't as much fun as it used to be. Worst of all, you've come to the sudden realization that you're not going to get a Christmas recess, and this has initiated a severe depression. You find yourself wishing you were back in school again, a sentiment you swore you'd never feel.

What's wrong? Well, you're more than likely a victim of the postcollege syndrome. This disease takes the form of a severe depression that strikes some recent graduates after they've been on the job for a few months. How do you know if you have this dread disease? Here are just some of the symptoms:

- You send away for dozens of graduate-school catalogs.
- You write term papers in your spare time.
- You give yourself an exam every few weeks.
- You secretly haunt your old dorm and college hangouts, trying to recapture your "lost" youth.
- You start donating half your paycheck to your college alumni fund.
- You start wearing your college sweatshirt (the one you never wore in school) to work.

If you feel any of these symptoms coming on, have no fear. The disease generally fades with time. Those "good old days" were probably not as golden as they suddenly seem. However, if you really get desperate, here are a few reminders of college reality guaranteed to eliminate most if not all of your nostalgia.

Remember . .

when you had to cram for finals and stuff tons of useless information into your head, only to forget it all one minute after the exam was over?

typing a twenty-page term paper at 8:30 A.M. because it was due at 9:00 A.M.?

trying to identify the thing on your dinner plate that the cafeteria wanted to pass off as food?

having to make up the results of a psychology lab experiment because the stupid mice didn't do what they were supposed to?

spending three hours on line trying to register for the next semester, only to discover you were closed out of the only course you really wanted to take?

having to explain to your parents that a course entitled "Love Poetry of the Nomadic Herdsmen" would one day come in handy?

Now, don't you feel a lot better?

Stress

Isn't stress something only middle-age male executives experience? No. It seems that almost every worker, no matter the age, sex, occupation, or position, is affected by stress. In fact, stress is a fact of working life. Actually, it's something you wouldn't want to eliminate altogether. You need some stress to function—be it a three o'clock deadline or the threat of losing your job. But what you do have to watch out for is the amount of it. Don't let it get out of hand. We all have our limits as far as strain goes. Once we exceed those limits, we hear from our bodies in the way of headaches, fatigue, stomach upsets, rapid heartbeat—you name it.

If you find yourself becoming overstressed, pinpoint the cause and try to eliminate it. It may be that your boss, knowing you're dependable, has heaped project upon project on your desk. Just the thought of attacking that pile of work has been giving you butterflies in your stomach. Plan on talking to your boss about it; let him or her know your limitations. He or she isn't a slave driver, and doesn't expect you to act like a superwoman. If you inform your boss of just how much you can do, he or she can change things accordingly.

But before you see your boss, come up with an alternative method for getting the work done. It may be a matter of distributing the work load among your coworkers. Most workers don't realize that it is in their power to delegate. They often confuse such action with shirking responsibility. Randy, a trainee at a brokerage firm, had the good fortune of having this spelled out to her by her boss. When he gave her a lengthy assignment, he told her, "I don't care how this gets done—I'm simply putting you in charge of seeing that it does." Your boss may have not given you such free reign. But he or she will be glad to listen to your proposition of hiring a temporary worker, or enlisting the help of your coworkers, to tackle those projects. The fact that you've been thinking of a remedy to the situation will make him or her aware of your concern.

As for handling occasional mild stress, try to keep a healthy sense of perspective about your work. When the phones are ringing off their cradles and you have three requests from three different people to fulfill, just remind yourself: "It's only business, and it won't help to get upset over it." Ask yourself what the worst that could happen would be. It's usually not so bad when you think in those terms. One woman on her first job says that whenever she starts feeling frazzled at work, she stops and asks herself: "What will this matter a hundred years from now?" This calms her down every time.

When you leave the office at night, make sure you leave

your problems there; don't take them home with you. Also, learn to make better use of your time during the day, so you'll have a sense of staying in control over your work. See the chapter on time management for a few tips.

Playing Hooky

We all have mornings when we wake up with the sun shining and the birds singing, and we're so happy that it's Saturday. But then we suddenly realize it's only Thursday and we're so angry we have to go to work, we're ready to scream bloody murder. The next time that happens to you, why not call in sick? It'll do you a world of good if every now and then you take a day off from work.

Try not to feel so guilty about doing it. Going to work day after day, week after week, can be a grind. And if you're fresh out of school, it may seem positively unbearable. However, this is not a tactic to be used often—after all, you should save your "sick" days for when you're really ill. But there are times when a letup is just what you may need. You may have had a particularly trying month at work, or perhaps there's a serious personal problem that's been on your mind. Going into work could only aggravate your emotional state. Remember that you have to maintain your emotional well-being. Your emotions too can make you ill if they are not heeded. You'll be surprised that after a day off from work, you'll actually look forward to going back the next day—and you'll probably be a better worker.

Boredom

At school, just when you'd start to get bored with a course, the semester would end. With unquestioned predictability, you'd be relieved from tedium about every fourteen weeks.

The work world doesn't operate in that fashion. You're not guaranteed much variety or stimulation in your assignments. And after chugging away at them for four, fourteen, or forty-two weeks, you may get bored—it's only natural.

What can you do to counteract boredom when it hits? Try to make the boring task unboring—create your own challenges. How? One way, learn the steps that precede your assignment and the steps that follow it. Carol Urbanski, a production head for a national boating magazine, notes that "It helps to get a full view of what you're doing, to see the other links, the other steps along the way." If, for instance, you always gather sales figures for your department's monthly report that gets drafted by Alice, ask your boss if this once you could write the report. Alice probably would appreciate a break from what has become for her a monotonous duty. Do let your boss know that you're becoming bored with what you're doing. He or she can only assume you're content unless told differently.

Another way to rid yourself of on-the-job boredom is to volunteer for new projects. Tackle organizing the file system in your office; ask to follow up on the year's delinquent accounts—there's no telling what you might learn from taking on tasks outside your usual scope.

If you find that you're still bored after having enlarged your assignments, or taken on additional ones, boredom may be a sign that it's time for you either to be promoted or to leave. When you find your boredom becoming a problem, it's wise to sit down and talk to your boss about your future.

Office Politics: Are All Those Stories True?

"I feel ill equipped to handle politics. I can't be cagey or manipulative, and I'm not good at game-playing."

"I'm aware of office politics, but I find I can't be 'devious.'"

Office politics. We asked some people to free-associate and tell us the first things that popped into their minds when they heard these two little words. Here are some of their replies:

Deceit — elitism — dog eat dog — gossip — hierarchies — cutthroats — phoniness — exploitation — cliques — getting stabbed in the back — sexual advances . . .

Hey, wait a minute! Are we talking about Watergate or office politics? Just what is this terrible thing, and is it catching?

Before we go on, let us say this: we will not moralize on the pros, cons, or perils of office politics. To the extent that it is a practice that exists within the work environment and that you will bump into sooner or later, you have to be aware of it. As one first-jobber wrote us: "I think the greatest service a book on first jobs could do would be to talk about office politics in a calm, offhand manner."

What is office politics and how does it work? In a nutshell, office politics can be defined as the competitive maneuvers used by workers to gain power, prestige, and promotion.

In most companies there is both a formal and an informal organization. The formal organization is the one you can put down on paper, where hierarchies and lines of communication can be clearly drawn. The informal organization is not as obvious, and it's also where most of the politicking will take place. As one bank vice president defined it for us, "Basically, office politics is who does what to whom and where and why; who lunches or teams up with whom; who really makes the decisions; who can I talk to who will talk to somebody else and say something that I need to get said; and who has the power and the inclination to help me move up."

If all this sounds confusing, it is. Maybe an analogy will help. Office politics is a little like playing Monopoly—with real money. Everyone maneuvers around the game board trying to pass "go" and keep out of "jail." In the process, players take risks, make deals with other players, buy and trade favors, and generally try to hoard enough money to buy Park Place and put three hotels on it. And just like Monopoly, the game of office politics is fraught with occasional setbacks. Power and money are apt to change hands quite a few times during the course of a usually *very* long game. The only certainty is that not everyone can win; who comes out ahead and when is often not determined until the very last move.

While most people will probably admit to enjoying the game of Monopoly, the same does not hold true for office politics. Being "political" at work has a terrible stigma attached to it. As Hennig and Jardim point out in *The Managerial Woman:* "Strategy now has a bad sound, a legacy of politicians who lost sight of moral objectives and adopted without question both the tenuous ethics of the game plan and a language drawn intact from the football field; men who took the concept of winning and made it an end in itself, never questioning the meaning of what they won since winning was enough in itself."

Competition. Strategy. Diplomacy. These are all essential elements of office politics. But for a generation raised on the Horatio Alger school of thought (i.e., work hard and you'll get ahead), discovering that working one's little tail off is not necessarily enough can be disheartening and disillusioning.

As one management development specialist told us, "I think one of the biggest problems I'm finding with people that come through the courses is understanding that things aren't that straight in business. It's very hard when you find that out. I know it was for me. You may be better than someone else, but that someone else has been around longer and . . . Politics can play a big part even though it's something that you can't 'see.'"

Coming to grips with the office political machine has proven to be even more difficult for women. We are all by now familiar with the theories that our socialization teaches us to be passive, nonassertive individuals. As a result we may be uncomfortable with power competition and risk-taking, overly sensitive to criticism, inflexible, and so on. To make matters even worse (could they possibly be worse?), as Hennig and Jardim point out, from the time they are sugar 'n spice 'n everything nice, little girls are taught that it's not whether you win or lose, it's how you play the game. When these "girls" are all grown up, they find that the rules have changed dramatically. It's *not* how you play the game, but whether you win or lose!

"So what are we supposed to do?" you ask. "It's too late to start climbing trees and playing football. Do I have to get caught up in all of this? Help!" Well, there are several schools of thought concerning office politics. One says you should just do your work and keep your nose clean. As the author of *Upward Nobility* put it, "You might also derive comfort from the fact that often it is the people who keep a low profile, stay out of politics, and coast along smoothly without making waves who are the ultimate survivors when kings rise and fall. I've seen it happen many times. . . ."

Another school believes that it's a business reality and fact of life that, of necessity, must be engaged in: "It would be great to avoid office politics altogether if that were possible. But capitalism encourages our competitive instincts, and business gives us an arena in which to manifest them. As long as there is business, there will be office politics." *(The New Executive Woman)*

Yet another group believes that it's an enjoyable process in and of itself. As one manager admitted to us, "To me, it's part of the spice of work."

Sorry, but we're not going to tell you which school of thought to believe, simply because what works for Jim and Susan in Company X might not work for you in Company Y. The degree and importance of office politics varies from company to company.

But to the extent that you'll be working with other people you'll be working within a political environment, because after all is said and done, politics *is* people. If you can learn to get along with a diverse group of workers with varying goals, personalities, and preferences, while maintaining your sanity and getting an occasional raise or promotion, you will have learned the most essential skill of the office politician—diplomacy. And diplomacy can make life a lot easier for everyone. Just ask any Nobel Peace Prize winner.

It's undeniable that many persons have pulled some pretty sneaky (cheap and dirty) moves going up the ladder. There *is,* however, a difference between dirty tricks and plain old strategy. "That's something that's not reinforced in women," according to career counselor Barbara Holt. "We're not supposed to be political. The feeling is that there's something not quite nice about developing strategy. Well, it's *darned* nice, it's great!"

Learn to differentiate among strategies early. Generally, they can be divided into three categories: Dirty Tricks, Questionable Maneuvers, and Clean Strategies.

For instance, Dirty Tricks would include the following:

- Deliberately withholding information from a colleague to his or her detriment and to your benefit.

- Spreading rumors about a colleague's personal life.

- Bad-mouthing a colleague's work behind his or her back.

Questionable Maneuvers include the following:

- Marrying the boss's daughter and becoming vice-president of the company.

- Marrying the boss's son and becoming vice-president of the company. (You don't get anything for just living with the boss's son/daughter.)

Examples of Clean Strategies are:

- Coming in to work early (and making sure someone finds out).

- Making certain your colleagues and/or superiors see you taking work home.

- Working late (and having the boss notice).

- Taking "important" people out to lunch (on you, of course).

- Identifying the type of behavior that is rewarded in your company (such as taking work home).

- Cultivating (and winning) the support of those in the company who are in a position to help you.

Obviously, you should not engage in *any* Dirty Tricks. It's not nice. Besides, you want to make it on your own strengths, not someone else's shortcomings.

Questionable Maneuvers are just that—questionable. For instance, suppose you divorce the boss's son/daughter? You may not remain vice-president for long. And you can't keep marrying your way into every company.

Clean Strategies are okay, in moderation. You can overdo these also. Someone who gets into work at 6:00 A.M. each and every morning and then manages to greet everybody else with a bright and chirpy "Oh, good morning! Is it nine already?" can become pretty annoying.

For those of you who are still sitting there saying you refuse to take any part in the game at all, fine. But be wary of falling into a victimization trap—*me* against *them*. You are not the only ethical, moral, sane, caring human being at work, and not everyone else is a despicable Machiavellian monster plotting and scheming to do you in.

"You have to understand how the game is played," said one bank officer. "I really resent the books that say the world is full of bastards and you have to learn to be a better one in order to be successful. Well, there are some bastards, but the point is that there are as many types of people at work as there are types of people. Categorization is narrow and self-defeating. Your situation, your role, and your responses can and should be more sophisticated and all-encompassing."

Whether you play the game or not and how you play it is a choice you alone will make. One thing is certain, though: don't get involved in it too early. Don't try to play without learning the rules. Sit and observe the people around you. Learn the workings of the business environment first.

One woman manager told us the advice she gives to new trainees: "Take with a grain of salt the things that people say to you. At first everyone will try to win you over, to make you go their way. What you have to decide is what is *your* way. Listen to what people are saying. Everyone's going to tell you their side of the story, but there are two sides to every story. Take the information and sort it out for yourself.

ATTENTION: WORKING MOTHERS

Lack of time and lack of energy are just two of the occupational hazards faced by working mothers. The Metropolitan Life Insurance Company offers a helpful booklet for women who are combining work and motherhood. "Mothers at Work" covers topics such as: sharing housework, parent-child relationships, and children's behavior. For a copy of the booklet and a list of other publications on personal and family health, child development, and safety write:

Health and Welfare Division
Metropolitan Life Insurance Company
One Madison Avenue
New York, N.Y. 10010

Part III

Skills and Strategies, or Learning What Everyone Assumes You Already Know

AS TIME GOES BY

8

WHAT DO IBM, The Bank of America, UNICEF, Exxon, the Ontario Ministry of Health, and Gloria Steinem have in common? Their unwavering dedication to the liberation of women? No. A Swiss bank account? No. (At least we don't know about it!) They all like disco music? No! No! The answer: They've all gone to top time management consultants for help in getting the most out of their valuable time.

Time management is a popular topic today. Seminars, workshops, books, and consultants all offer help to individuals and organizations in making the best use of their work and leisure time. Since you've heard about how time flies and that time and tide wait for no man (or woman), and everyone knows that time's a wastin', that time is money, and that a stitch in time saves nine, let's not forget that lost time is never found again. And since time is of the essence, use the advice given in this chapter to help you manage your time.

Making Plans

If you want to make the best use of your time, you first must do a little planning. According to Alan Lakein, the well known time-management consultant, the first step is to identify your goals—both short and long term. What does goal-setting have to do with time management? You won't be able to make the best use of your time unless you figure out what the best use of it is! Stating your goals can clarify what's important to you, where you are going, and how you want to get there. Only then can you set aside the time to accomplish the things of value to you.

By goals we don't mean general statements like, "I want to be rich." Your goals should be specific and concrete statements of what you want to achieve. For instance: "I want to learn French by the end of the year," or "I want to complete the credits for my degree this coming semester."

Since some goals will be more important to you than others, and since you want to make the best use of your time, you must establish priorities. Priorities can help you concentrate on what's really important to you. Lakein's time-management system assigns an A, B, C value to goals—A for the big-value ones, B for medium value, and C for low value. (He suggests that you forget the C's completely and concentrate on the A's and B's.) Whether you rank them 1, 2, 3 or A, B, C, it's important that you sit and think about *your* priorities.

Next, write down specific steps you must take to achieve these goals. For instance, suppose you want to get the necessary credits to finish your degree. Your first step might be to get a course catalogue; next to decide what courses you have to take, then to register for them, and so on. Or suppose you want to update your résumé. One step would be sitting down and listing all your accomplishments during the past six months on the job; the next step would be revising and rewriting the résumé, and finally making some copies of the finished product. These "action" steps can be incorporated into your daily schedule, thus bringing you closer to achieving your goals.

It's important that you review and revise your goals list periodically, because goals will change as you grow and develop. As your values, experiences, and aspirations change, some goals will become more important to you, or less. So keep your list up to date.

You can use basically the same system to plan your daily schedule. Most time-management experts agree that a daily *To Do* list—an inventory of all the important tasks you plan to do during a given day—is the key to efficient use of time. A *To Do* list can also keep your work schedule from becoming too hectic. As Portia Manley, a marketing analyst with the Weyerhaeuser Company, says, "If I plan out each week, and a big project comes up, I can see what I'm doing and I can set my priorities. That alleviates a lot of stress." When writing your *To Do* list, consultants suggest you eliminate routine tasks such as showering, making breakfast, etc., and concentrate on the things you want to and must do that might not otherwise get done.

Some tips for your *To Do* list:

- Many experts advise that you use a specific time for writing your list daily. Take time when you arrive at work in the morning (or the night before) to plan your schedule. Keep both long- and short-term goals in mind. Write down all your goals and tasks on one list; otherwise you'll waste lots of time just looking for the lists! Keep your *To Do* list short and specific.

- Since you will probably have more items on your list than you could accomplish in one day, set priorities in your *To Do* list. Which tasks are the most urgent or have the greatest value for you? Keep in mind any meetings or deadlines already on your agenda. Rank your To Do's and then *do them in that order.* This rule is an important one, because otherwise you'll be tempted to concentrate on easy or nonessential tasks instead of the truly important ones.

• Don't schedule every minute of your day, because (a) unexpected meetings, visitors, or assignments will come up that might take precedence over your *To Do* list, and (b) you need time to breathe and relax, otherwise you'll go bananas!

• When scheduling your day, take account of your biorhythm. There are certain periods of the day when your energy reserves are at their highest. Are you a morning, afternoon, or night person? As Stephanie Winston suggests in her book *The Organizing Principle,* "You can check your own biorhythm by briskly exercising for five minutes in the morning and again late in the afternoon. If you feel exhausted in the morning and invigorated in the afternoon, you may be a night person; if it's the other way around, you're probably a morning person. Check your mental faculties as well. Work half of a challenging crossword puzzle in the morning and try the other half in the afternoon. Can you detect a difference in acuity?"

Make your body work *with* you. Schedule important tasks and those that require great concentration or imagination for the time when your energy levels are at their highest. Routine tasks can be scheduled for periods when your energy level is medium to low. Learn to identify your own "rhythm" so that you can use it to your best advantage.

The Mañana Syndrome

> Procrastination is the thief of time.
>> Edward Young, *Night Thoughts (Night I)*

Procrastination is one of the biggest time-wasters of all. It is also one of the biggest sources of anxiety, since we usually procrastinate doing the "Have To" tasks that are unpleasant, boring, or seemingly overwhelming and complicated. Then we worry because they haven't been done yet! There's that report the boss wants and for which you'll have to dig through all the old, dusty files. Or that meeting you have to set up that will require at least thirteen phone calls. Or that report you have to write.

It's difficult to find the motivation to do these Have Tos—after all, if they were Want Tos, you wouldn't have a problem. But there are some steps you can take to overcome terminal procrastination:

- Salami and cheese, anyone? Time-management consultants seem to have a fondness for food analogies. One system for curing procrastination is variously referred to as the Swiss Cheese Technique or the Salami Technique. We call it the Food Technique. Basically, it means breaking up large or unpleasant tasks into smaller, more easily manageable components. In other words, "poking holes" (Swiss cheese) into large tasks, or "slicing" them (salami) into smaller bits (bites?). Look through just *one* of those dusty, old files; make just *one* of those thirteen phone calls; write one paragraph instead of the entire report. You may find that it isn't such an unpleasant or complex task. And taking it a bit at a time can also help you get (and keep) your momentum going.

- Set a deadline for yourself and then tell someone else about it. Do a little bragging. That way, if you don't come through, you'll be terribly embarrassed! (One caveat: be realistic in assessing the time needed to complete a task. Everyone has a different work pace. Setting unrealistic deadlines will only further increase your anxiety and lead to even more procrastination.)

- Reward yourself. Promise yourself a "present" if you get the task (or part of it) completed. The present can be anything you like—from a fifteen-minute work break to a movie, a new book, a nice lunch— something you really want or would like to do.

- As a last resort, wait until an even worse assignment comes along. It might make the one you're procrastinating on now seem pretty easy by comparison!

Working the "Garbage Detail"

Have you ever spent endless minutes looking for a file you *know* is in the office somewhere, and can't find? Does all the incoming paper seem to land in your *In* box and never make it out? Do you have to fight the stacks of paper on your desk just to find someplace to put your elbows?

Excessive clutter can be a real time-waster on the job. Some people spend so much time *pushing* paper around that they never actually get around to *doing* anything. What can be done? Subject your work area to a periodic purge. If you cannot be organized on a daily basis, the periodic purge is the next best thing. It's your chance to rid your work area of all its accumulated junk and paper. If you are highly industrious, you will do this once a week. (If you're not, at least try for every other week.)

The top of your desk should be visible. (When have you last seen it?) Eliminate all unnecessary junk that may have accumulated. Take all the papers in your *In* box and any others accumulated elsewhere on the desk and divide them into three piles:

- *To Do,* or *Action,* pile
- *To File* pile
- *Junk* pile

Remember the old saying, "A diamond is a girl's best friend?" Well, a wastebasket is a career woman's best friend. Be ruthless when sorting out paper. Throw out as much as possible. Take action on the *To Do* pile immediately if possible. If not, as a reminder, leave it visible and within arm's reach.

Your desk drawers should be used to keep the supplies you most often need to do your work. No law says that they must be filled to the brim. If your drawers are a combination stationer's/candy store/pharmacy, it's time to eliminate some junk. Take *everything* out of the drawer and examine it critically—can it be thrown away? (Answer "yes" as often as you can.)

Subject your files to the same periodic purge. There's a difference between filing and hoarding (insects hoard, people file). Most files over a year old are generally never looked at. Make an "active" pile of the files you very frequently need and keep them in a section toward the front of your filing cabinet. Learn to be critical of papers that you file. In this age of excess photocopying, we are tempted to save more paper than is necessary. Don't get caught up in a paper chase.

How to Get to Work on Time

Some workers undergo short periods of chronic lateness. They may be under pressure at work, be having difficulties with a colleague, or be working on a particularly tough assignment. Coming in late can postpone dealing with these problems. Some people are always late because they hate or are bored with their jobs. Just the thought of walking into the office is enough to make them roll over and sleep for another hour. For those people the best solution might lie in finding another job.

But then there are those who just can't seem to get it together in the morning. They like their jobs but hate to get up. Somehow they never seem to have anything to wear, every pair of pantyhose they own has runs, they never have change for the bus, and the car keys have mysteriously disappeared.

For anyone who falls into this last category, here are some tips to help you get off to a good (and early) start in the morning:

- Buy a clock radio that has a back-up alarm—the radio comes on, and ten or fifteen minutes later a buzzer goes off that won't stop unless you turn it off. (It's usually very annoying.) Try placing whatever alarm you have on a piece of furniture that's out of arm's reach. Perhaps if you have to get up physically and walk to turn the darn thing off, you might stay up!

- If alarms don't do the trick, try hiring a professional wake-up service. Look in the Yellow Pages under "Wake-Up Call Service." (The Manhattan Yellow Pages revealed these gems: "No Sleep Is Too Deep— We'll Wake You" and "Wake Up to a Pleasant Voice—Call Us for Surprises"!) These services guarantee to wake you up no matter what. Some even give you the morning weather report.

If you can't afford one, talk a friend into being your service. (Make sure you pick a friend who doesn't have a problem waking up.) Buy him or her dinner in exchange. Make him or her promise to keep ringing until you do wake up. You promise not to hate your friend for doing it!

• Sit down for a minute and make a list of all the things you'll need tomorrow morning. For instance:

Clothes you plan to wear
Handbag
Briefcase
Car/house keys
Change for the bus/train
Shoes and stockings

Try assembling all this gear the night before. Decide what you want to wear and make certain it's clean and wrinkle-free. Get out your shoes and put whatever stockings or socks you'll wear in them. Pack your handbag and briefcase and leave them near the front door. Put your house/car keys near them. (If you're always losing keys, consider getting a small hook to put in the kitchen or your bedroom. Force yourself to hang your keys there whenever they are not in use.) If you use public transportation, make certain you have the correct change. (You could buy yourself one of those little dime-store change dispensers. When you cash your paycheck, get a week's worth of travel change and put it in the dispenser. That way you're always sure of having some.

• Don't dawdle with the newspaper over breakfast. It's nice to read the paper in the morning, but if you're a slow starter, it will take up valuable time. Save it for the train, for lunch, or the evening.

Eat something quick and easy for breakfast. For instance: toast, yogurt, cereal, cottage cheese. Save the eggs benedict or pancakes for leisurely weekend breakfasts. Skip the second cup of coffee—you probably don't need all that caffeine anyway.

• To keep your momentum going, try writing down a schedule for yourself to follow in the morning. For instance: 6:30–6:45—roll out of bed; 6:45–7:00—shower; etc. If you're really desperate, buy an egg timer and time yourself to make sure you stick to your schedule. Another technique is to turn on one of those all-news radio stations that give you the time every fifteen minutes or so.

• If you rely on public transportation, get schedules or time the service yourself. Aim for the bus or train that will get you to work ahead of time.

TIME TIPS FROM THE PROS

When you realize that you are procrastinating on a major task, slice it up into as many small, manageable "instant tasks" as possible. Promise yourself that you won't force yourself to get involved with the main job, provided you do at least one of the small steps on your list.

> EDWIN C. BLISS,
> *Getting Things Done: The
> A B C's of Time Management*

Be decisive. Don't be so afraid of making a mistake that you do nothing. "Success," it has been said, "consists of being right 51 percent of the time." Once you have all the pertinent facts before you, therefore, reach a decision and act. And once you have acted, don't waste time in fruitless speculation over the wisdom of your decision. Go on to other things.

> TED POLLOCK, Ph.D., *Managing Yourself Creatively*

Hold every moment sacred. Give each clarity and meaning, each the weight of thine awareness, each its true and due fulfillment.

> THOMAS MANN, *The Beloved Returns*

The demands on your time will continue to multiply unless you weigh carefully those things you very much want to do and say "no," nicely, to the countless other requests. You will respect yourself more when you begin to feel in control of your time.

> DONNA GOLDFEIN
> *Everywoman's Guide to Time
> Management*

For time lost may nought recovered be.

> GEOFFREY CHAUCER, *Troilus and Criseyde*

Try not to put down an incoming piece of paper that requires a response until you have fired off that response. It is often easier to think of the right thing to say when you've just received the letter and your first reaction is fresh in your mind.

ALAN LAKEIN,
*How to Get Control of Your
Time and Your Life*

Early to bed and early to rise, makes a [wo]man healthy, wealthy, and wise.

BENJAMIN FRANKLIN, *Poor Richard's Almanac*

Plan small projects during waiting periods. Outline a report or pay bills while sitting in the doctor's office; polish silver while clothes are in the dryer; pick out a birthday card between appointments; make up the bed while waiting for the water to boil; make out your shopping list while riding on the bus. Most small chores can be accomplished in bits and pieces of time.

STEPHANIE WINSTON, *The Organizing Principle*

Know the resources available to you. Know where you can go for help when you need it—who has what skill, who has slack time at the moment; what staff specialists are available to help.

MARGARET HIGGINSON and
THOMAS QUICK,
*The Ambitious Woman's Guide
to a Successful Career*

Curtsy while you're thinking what to say. It saves time.
The Queen of Hearts

LEWIS CARROLL, *Alice's Adventures in Wonderland*

TIME TIPS FROM SOME NONPROS

We asked the busy Catalyst staff for their time-saving tips. Here are some of their suggestions:

1. Group all phone calls together between 10 and 12 A.M. It's the best time to reach most people.
2. Don't leave messages for people to call back. You get back to them; otherwise you are constantly interrupted.
3. Catch up on reading while traveling by bus or train.
4. Make use of office intercom systems. Don't walk all around to reach people; it's a time-waster.
5. Delegate as much as possible—even at home. Have things delivered, order by phone. It saves time.
6. If you're working on a project and people come by your office to chat (business or pleasure), ask if you can get back to them within a specific amount of time. Same thing with phone calls.
7. Put aside non-urgent problems. When you get to deal with them, they may already have solved themselves. (But be careful in choosing "non-urgents.")
8. Ask the receptionist at the front desk (or your secretary) to hold calls and take messages.
9. When you can, put a sign on your door—"Do Not Disturb."
10. Do what the boss needs *first*.
11. Hit the ground running when you come in. Don't waste time with coffee, gossip, sharpening pencils, or "getting ready" to work.
12. Make lots of lists. When something *must* be done, *do* it!
13. Keep a clean desk with no piles of paper.
14. Do your banking by mail—it saves a lot of waiting-in-line time.
15. Buy several birthday, anniversary, congratulations, etc., cards at a time. That way you'll have one if there's no time to go out and buy one.
16. Use Friday afternoon (when you're generally pooped-out) to throw out all the junk and papers that have accumulated in your office during the week.

HOW CAN YOU MANAGE HOME AND JOB? TIME TIPS FOR THE HARRIED HOMEMAKER

Combining work and family responsibilities requires careful, thoughtful planning. Somehow—in your own style—you *do* have to be efficient. There are just so many hours in one day, and time for a job outside your home may have to fit into an already nearly full schedule.

Your home may run very efficiently now, but when you start working, you will have to be even more organized. You will learn as you go how to use your time more effectively, and you will probably be surprised at how rapidly you get things done. If you are a newcomer to the business of combining raising a family and pursuing a career, you probably need some suggestions about how this complicated effort can be done effectively so that it brings satisfaction and enrichment to your life. Here are some ideas that have served other women and may also help you:

- Plan ahead: cluster your errands according to neighborhood; plan weekly menus in advance; cook double quantities and freeze half; market just once a week.

- Delegate chores and responsibilities to your children and your husband, and employ domestic or maintenance help if you can afford it. Keep a list of who's doing what and when. Don't be afraid to hand over jobs to your children. Even a five-year-old can set the table, pick up toys, make the bed, and feed the animals.

- Write down all family time commitments (medical appointments, PTA meetings, ballet classes, etc.) on *one* calendar that is strategically located (for instance, in the den or kitchen) so that everyone can see it and plan ahead.

- Conduct less business or other formal entertaining at home. All of it may not be essential, so reduce or eliminate what you can. Talk it over with your family and decide where and how you can make changes.

- Take a critical look at your social life. Can some events or activities be altered? Are some parts of your informal social life mechanical—or even boring? Could they be eliminated?

- If you have been active in a variety of community affairs, set priorities there as well. You may choose to cut back on many activities or to concentrate on the one or two that mean the most to you and your family. Try to measure how much time you can and want to give to community work, considering the importance of your personal contribution and how many others may be available to take your place.

  Finally, consider the possibility that everything does not have to be done perfectly or exactly on time. The world won't end if your home isn't spotless. Your kids won't turn into juvenile delinquents if you make them work around the house. Trying to transform yourself into Superwoman will only make life miserable for you and for your family because it is impossible. You can't be all things to all people at all times. Your energy and enthusiasm have natural limits. Keep in mind that you will want time for the lazy, self-indulgent part of you (yes, *you)* that enjoys a leisurely weekend or likes to talk with friends or write letters or read or play tennis or watch TV. Do yourself and your family a favor by keeping a little time for yourself.

9

COMMUNICATING WITH OTHERS

ONE OF THE primary ways of communicating with others on the job involves writing. If you thought your writing days were over when you handed in your last term paper, guess again. Memos, letters, and reports to write are all lying in wait for you at this very moment. And your first job is likely to unleash some of these demons.

"Writing is an extremely important job skill—in almost any job," said one trainer at a life insurance company. "Anything you write is there for people who don't know you to see." Business relationships are often conducted solely via the written word. What you say and how you say it will convey an impression of both you, the writer, and your company. "Bosses are fairly tolerant of the fact that a lot of employees have to be trained in writing skills," said one manager, "but if you can come to them from the beginning with pretty good skills, they'll really appreciate it."

Writing to Be Read

There is no golden rule of writing; no formula for creativity. Keats or Shelley may have relied on his muse for inspiration, but unfortunately, most of us aren't as blessed.

Those of you who shudder at the mere sight of paper and pencil should take heart: becoming a competent writer requires no magic or overwhelming literary talent—just practice.

Memos:
    are a nuisance to write
    are a nuisance to read
    waste time
    waste paper
    clutter up your *In* box
    often contain unnecessary information

The above was obviously written by someone who hates to read (and write) memos. However, in some offices, memo-writing is a required (yes and even useful) skill. If you're one of a cast of thousands where you work, a well written memo might be a method of getting your supervisor's attention—and time. A memo can be an effective means of conveying and protecting your ideas. Memos can be routed to several persons at once, all of whom will come to the simultaneous realization that they have a budding genius in their midst. In some companies, in fact, employees seem to communicate *only* via the memo route; there interpretation of the memo becomes a fine art in itself. ("Now, what did she *really* mean by that memo?")

While memos can have a useful purpose, some people do love memo-writing for its own sake. They are the memo monsters—they'll write a memo inviting you to lunch in fifteen minutes, or to say good night at the end of the day! This exaggeration notwithstanding, almost everyone has to write a memo at some time in his or her career. When your time comes, try to keep the memo short and to the point. Remember those ideas you may have picked up in creative writing class? Well, now is *not* the time to use them. Memos are not the place to include all the literary allusions, similes, metaphors, or any other linguistic tricks you have at your disposal. And, if you find that you're resorting to a thesaurus to find a bigger word when a simple one will do, you are sadly deficient in the art of memo-writing.

We've taken liberties with a well known literary passage to illustrate some of the do's and dont's of memo-writing. (Our apologies to our former English professors.) The first version of the memo illustrates what the principals involved actually had to say. The second version illustrates how the memo should have been written.

Example #1
(Memo regarding what's in a name)

> To my dear Romeo,
> What's in a name? that which we call a rose
> By any other name would smell as sweet;
> So Romeo would, were he not Romeo call'd,
> Retain that dear perfection which he owes
> Without that title. Romeo, doff thy name;
> And for that name, which is no part of thee,
> Take all myself.
>
> From
> Juliet

Example #2

May 21, 1584

MEMO

To: Romeo Montague

From: Juliet Capulet

Subject: Your present title

I have learned that certain members of the organization find your present title, "Office Romeo," inappropriate.

Although you and I agree that titles are essentially unimportant, in the interest of maintaining a good working relationship, I suggest we meet to discuss a suitable alternative.

Please get back to me this afternoon to arrange the time and place.

cc: Friar Lawrence
    Mr. Capulet
    Mr. Montague

Memo #1 contains far too many ruffles and flourishes. Ms. Capulet, intent on exhibiting her literary talents, arrives at her point in a very roundabout way. She concludes (after much meandering) that Romeo must get rid of his name; however, she offers no suggestions as to how or when this should be accomplished. Romeo is left unsure of what action, if any, he is to take. The memo also uses an incorrect format and is not dated.

Memo #2, however, is a much better way to communicate when dealing with business. The correct format is used, including the date, "To," "From," Subject, and the first and last names of both sender and recipient. It is precise and to the point. Ms. Capulet wastes no words; she makes clear what action she expects from Romeo and when. Carbon copies are sent to those in the organization who are directly involved or have some interest in the matter. (Shakespeare may have had a certain flair with words, but he would never have made it in the business world!)

A few more things about memos: some companies have preprinted memo forms; in that case, you don't have to worry about format. When you send a group memo, check to see if names are usually listed alphabetically, according to seniority, or in any other "style." Look in back files and your colleagues' *In* boxes for clues. If you work in a large office, it might be a good idea to hand-deliver any urgent memos, rather than relying on interoffice mail.

Business Letters

Clarity and brevity should be the hallmarks of a good business letter. Unfortunately, these two words are foreign to many of today's letter writers. Here are some guidelines for writing effective business letters:

- Decide exactly what you want to say. A business letter should get to the point quickly. If you're on the third paragraph and still trying to decide what the point is, start over. There's nothing more annoying than having to wade through a lot of sentences before finding out why someone has written to you. So get to the point as soon as possible.

- Write it the way you'd say it. It's amazing how many people can sound perfectly coherent in conversation, yet become mired in confusing vocabulary and outdated phrasing when writing a business letter. They are victims of "jargonese," a widespread disease. They substitute the elaborate phrase for the simple one; the ornate word for the plain one. They use hackneyed, trite expressions in a futile attempt to make their letters sound profound or intricate. They write letters that are fifteen sentences long, when five would do. The results of "jargonese" are vague, wordy letters that are boring to read and often make little sense to anyone but the sender.

   The following is an example of a letter sadly infected by "jargonese":

Dear Mr. Smith:

   In accordance with your request, I am herewith enclosing our report entitled: "Jargonese Is a Disease."

Despite the fact that at the present writing the aforementioned report is under revision, the consensus of opinion is that it will provide you with a complete overview of the basic fundamentals.

In the event that this edition does not meet with your approval, please notify this writer and I will send you a revised copy at the earliest possible moment.

Allow me to express our appreciation for your interest in this matter.

Sincerely,

Sandra Kaufmann

It's enough to make you gag, isn't it? As Strunk and White point out in *The Elements of Style:* "Rich ornate prose is hard to digest, generally unwholesome, and sometimes nauseating." How true.

What can be done to save this letter from the ravages of "jargonese"? Simplify. You don't have to resort to writing sentences like "See Jane run." But you must eliminate unnecessary words and tired phrasing. For instance: "In accordance with your request" should be "As you requested"; "despite the fact that" can be substituted with a simple "although." Here is the complete version of the "cured" letter:

Dear Mr. Smith:

As you requested, here is our report "Jargonese Is a Disease."

Although we are revising it, we think this edition covers the fundamentals of business writing. If you'd like to receive the revised version, we'll send it as soon as it is ready.

Thanks for your interest in our project.

Sincerely,

Sandra Kaufmann

Five words to avoid at all costs are *forthwith, heretofore, herewith, aforementioned,* and *hereto.* They are stuffy, archaic, and sound silly to boot. If you have heretofore used any of these aforementioned words, you will herewith refrain from doing so forthwith.

Other phrases to steer clear of (we have suggested substitutions in parentheses): *due to the fact that* and *in view of the fact that (since); in order that (so); at the present time (now); in the event that (if); with regard to (about); I am taking the liberty of writing (I am writing).* Unfortunately nineteenth-century wordiness still plagues some modern business correspondence. A quick look through any filing cabinet in your office would probably produce a few prime examples.

More advice on improving your business writing:

• Don't use the editorial "we," unless you are really speaking for the entire company. Use "I" instead.

• Use paragraphs to break up the letter into easily readable units. Business letters that look like one giant mass of typewriting are difficult to read. Paragraph as often as necessary so that your letter reads smoothly. A paragraph that's only two sentences is fine. Use punctuation (hyphens, colons, semicolons, etc.) to help make your sentences short and direct.

• Proofread. This step is a very important one. Make certain that you have the correct name and address of the person you are writing to. Whether you or someone else types the letter, take a few extra minutes to check for stylistic, grammatical, or typographical errors. You won't create a very favorable impression if the letters you send are full of typos, smudges, or misspelled words.

• End the letter when you've said everything necessary. If you've covered all the pertinent information in three sentences, don't try to "cushion" the letter with extra words or phrases. This tactic only leads to "jargonese" and won't necessarily make the letter better, just longer. Whenever you're tempted to fatten up a letter, remember these lines of Alexander Pope's:

> Words are like leaves; and where they most abound,
> Much fruit of sense beneath is rarely found.

• Try to answer within forty-eight hours any correspondence you receive; such promptness makes a good impression and keeps your desk neat.

If you are having problems composing business letters, try reading letters in back files. Study letters that you receive. Don't copy them exactly, but as you become acquainted with the general tone of business correspondence, you'll soon develop a style of your own.

Reports

When writing a relatively long report, take time to think it out in your head first. Decide what your main point will be, and group all subordinate ideas around it. If you can't see what the focus of your writing is, your reader won't either.

Make rough outlines; jot down ideas as they occur to you. Be specific and direct; try to give examples that will illustrate general principles. Any data you include should support your theme and make your argument stronger.

No rule of writing states that you must begin with the first sentence and write all the way to the last one. Some writers write in "pieces," beginning in the middle or end, and then pull it together. Some wait for "inspiration" to strike. Others sit and grind it out, inspiration notwithstanding. Everyone has her/his own style. You should work in the one that's most comfortable and effective for you.

After you've finished a draft of any piece of writing, set it aside for a while. Then put yourself in the reader's place and review your work critically:

Is the main point clear?

Can you understand it all the way through?

Are there any sections, sentences, or words that you have to read twice to grasp? Any words you don't understand?

How can the writing be improved?

Take time to revise and rewrite. The care you put into your writing will be evident in the end product.

You Are What You Say

"The first time I had to give a speech was one of the more nerve-wracking moments in my life. I was standing in front of what seemed to be a thousand pairs of beady eyes just staring at me; waiting for me to say something terribly significant—or stupid! My mouth felt as if I'd swallowed a box of chalk."

As we see from this quotation, the art of speaking—and of speaking up—does not come easily to many people. But when you think about it, all of us engage in public speaking in one form or another all the time. Whether it's arguing with the butcher, debating an issue at a PTA meeting, or trying to persuade a professor to extend the deadline on a term paper, we're always giving speeches. But when the art of speaking becomes a little more formalized—for instance, speaking in front of an "audience" of any size—many of us blanch with fear and head for the nearest exit.

Many women seem to have a particularly difficult time learning to speak up—to assert themselves and communicate effectively via the spoken word. And it's no wonder: as little girls we were taught that to be soft-spoken and demure was to be "feminine." It wasn't "nice" to speak too loudly or too aggressively. Gentility was the name of the game.

Boys, however, were taught a different lesson. From the time they were grubby peewees in football jerseys, boys learned that speaking up—speaking out—was the easiest way to get ahead. Most men seem to have learned their lessons very well.

Unfortunately, most women have learned their lessons only too well—to keep quiet. In *Language and Woman's Place,* Robin Lakoff points out that

> The ultimate effect of these discrepancies is that women are systematically denied access to power, on the grounds that they are not capable of holding it, as demonstrated by their linguistic behavior along with other aspects of their behavior; and the irony here is that women are made to feel that they deserve such treatment, because of inadequacies in their own intelligence and/or education. But in fact it is precisely because women have learned their lessons so well that they later suffer such discrimination.

The fact is that speaking *is* power—the power to assert yourself, to voice your opinions, to defend your rights; the power to make a *contribution* in any sphere of life. And whether you're attempting to "sell" yourself at a job interview or to describe a new project idea to your boss and coworkers, good speaking skills are an essential prerequisite for success on the job. Public speaking is a skill that *can* be learned—by doing it. It's a skill that must be practiced—

often—to perfect it. It can't really be learned by reading a book. We'll give you a few guidelines that can help you improve your speaking habits, but you must go out and put these guidelines into use.

Lack of role models, lack of encouragement, and lack of opportunity have kept women silent for too long. It's high time we learned to speak up. Feminist Lucy Stone spoke up at the 1885 Women's Rights Convention. At a time when women speaking in public were an object of curiosity (and scorn), Lucy Stone "spoke" her mind:

> The capacity to speak indicates the right to do so, and the noblest, highest and best thing that any one can accomplish, is what that person ought to do, and what God holds him or her accountable for doing.

How Do I Sound?

Many of our interactions with other people are vocal ones. One way that people form an impression of us is by listening to our speech. In this respect, *how* we say something is as important as *what* we're saying. Many research studies have been conducted to examine how our speech habits can affect the way people perceive us. For instance, in *First Impressions: The Psychology of Encountering Others,* Chris Kleinke describes the results of one study that showed that people tend to associate certain stereotypes with various voice qualities:

> Males with breathiness in their voices were seen as younger and more artistic. Females with breathiness gave the impression of being pretty, feminine, petite, high-strung, and shallow. Flatness in the voice was associated with masculinity, sluggishness, and coldness in both males and females. Nasality was perceived as largely undesirable. Males with

tenseness in their voice were evaluated as older, unyielding, and cantankerous. Females with tense voices came across as young, emotional, high-strung, and less intelligent. Increased rate of speaking made both males and females appear animated and extroverted. Increased pitch variety gave males a dynamic, feminine, and aesthetically inclined identification. Females with a wide pitch variety appeared dynamic and extroverted.

Tone and rate of speech aren't the only factors that can affect how others perceive you. Your body language also serves to reinforce what you're saying and how others receive your message. If your eyes are constantly shifting around nervously while you're speaking, you may appear anxious or untrustworthy; if you're standing hunched over or are constantly fiddling around with your hair or earrings, you can "sound" irresponsible, bored, scared—or all of the above.

Since your speech habits can leave a lasting impression on people, it's important to recognize your own speaking habits so that you can work toward overcoming any problems. How? Give yourself a speech—talk into a tape recorder or stand in front of a mirror and give a short talk. Better yet, get some friends or family members to be your "audience" and have them offer a critique of you afterward.

Often you may not be aware of your own body language; in such a case others can pinpoint problems much more readily. For instance, maybe you're unconsciously tapping your feet or grabbing at your necklace; maybe you're flapping your arms so hard that you look as if you're going to take flight. You may also be unaware that you're using incorrect grammar or too many slang expressions. You may be speaking too quickly or hesitating too often. Too many "you knows," "likes," or "uhms" may be scattered in your speech. Friends and tape recorders are useful in pointing out vocal and body language "mistakes."

Becoming aware of any problems is the first step, but practice can help you develop speech habits that are comfortable and effective.

Speeches

> "Then you should say what you mean," the March Hare went on.
> "I do," Alice hastily replied; "at least—at least I mean what I say—that's the same thing, you know."
> "Not the same thing a bit!" said the Hatter. "Why, you might just as well say that 'I see what I eat' is the same thing as 'I eat what I see'!"
>
> *Alice's Adventures in Wonderland*

You've been chosen to give a presentation on the latest "gizmo" your company is manufacturing. The audience will be full of out-of-town salespeople who know nothing about you or the new product. Before your legs turn to mush and you grab the fastest plane to Siberia, remind yourself that this is your golden opportunity to shine. Everyone can get "through" a speech; but by keeping a few guidelines in mind, you will not only get "through" it, you will also give a good, informative speech. And you might even enjoy doing it!

Preparation and practice are the two basic ingredients of a good speech. Before making any type of speech or presentation, you must be thoroughly familiar with your topic. The interest you take in your subject will be reflected by the interest your audience takes in you.

Most experts suggest that you outline your speech. Jot down the main ideas in sequence and flesh them out as you give your talk. Memorized or written speeches tend to sound mechanical—and boring. However, remember that the best technique is the one that's best for *you*. One first-jobber told us that for her, "It's absolutely essential that I write down everything I want to say, otherwise I become too nervous thinking I'll forget to say something. I try not to actually memorize the speech but to read it as naturally as possible. It takes practice, but it's what works for me."

Rehearse your speech beforehand. The more comfortable you are with your material, the more comfortable you'll feel in front of an audience. It's best if you can practice in front of a "captive" audience—friends or family who can give you feedback on your performance. But as first-jobber Debbie told us, "Mirrors are pretty good audiences too. I gave my first 'speech' to my bathroom mirror. It may sound silly, but it helped me to practice my eye contact and get used to hearing myself talk. It's really important to 'say' your speech out loud, because sometimes words that look great on paper sound funny or awkward in the context of a speech."

Whatever the occasion, make sure that your clothing is appropriate and comfortable. You won't be able to concentrate on what you're saying if you're worried that your clothes are too tight or if your shoes are killing your feet. Avoid wearing dangling jewelry that can become tangled on microphones and make a lot of noise.

Before you give your speech, take a few deep breaths— and relax! "It helps to keep reminding yourself that you know more about your subject than the audience does," says Andrea, another first-jobber new to the speaking game. "After all, that's why *you're* the speaker! Don't underestimate your audience; assume that they are interested in listening to what you have to say."

If no one is on hand to present you, introduce yourself to the audience and tell a little about your background: why you are qualified to talk about your subject. Set the tone at the beginning of your talk. If you're comfortable with humor, you can begin with an anecdote or a humorous quotation. However, if you don't have a funny bone in your entire body, don't try to become Gilda Radner overnight. A "funny-thing-happened-to-me-on-the-way-to-this-speech" story can be embarrassing to you and to your audience if it's not told with a technique that's part of your own personal style.

Also, avoid trying out any unusual or phony gestures that you've concocted for the special occasion. If they don't come naturally, they will just look awkward. You don't have to turn yourself into a "perfect" speaker; you want to sound natural. Warmth and credibility will count for more than twenty perfect gestures will.

Develop your point logically. Back up your statements with facts, and try to keep overwhelming or confusing statistics to a minimum. Remember to make your language clear and concise and avoid using clichés or slang. Keeping your tone conversational is best.

Muriel Fox, executive vice-president of the public relations agency Carl Byoir and Associates and president of its subsidiary, MediaCom Communications Training, offers the following tips for effective speechmaking:

- Always ask yourself what's in it for your listeners, why are they here, and what do they hope to get out of it. Couch what you have to say as much as you can in terms of their self-interest.

- State your conclusions up front. Tell them, in other words, where you're going, where you plan to bring them out at the end.

- Always accentuate the positive. Audiences are not interested in problems; more likely they are there to hear answers and solutions.

- If you are selling an organization, or a service, be sure to tell them how well you're doing; drop names whenever you can—names of influential people who share your views, have used your service, or solicited your advice.

• Anticipate negative questions, and practice how to answer them in advance. Never ignore an accusation or criticism, but be succinct in addressing it, then move quickly to a positive.

• Don't be afraid to be too simple in describing your service or topic. Assume that most people in the audience don't know anything about you, and are only half listening anyway.

• Use illustrations and anecdotes whenever possible. People enjoy hearing about how others like them have behaved.

• Tricks for relating well to an audience: (1) Single listeners out: talk directly to one individual, then another. (2) You can grab them by speaking louder, or softer, by using your hands, or better yet, your whole body. Remember, the point is to grab and hold their attention throughout. (3) Use language that's colorful, not abstract. (4) Be humorous whenever you can *comfortably*.

• Don't distribute any printed material until after your speech. Otherwise they'll be going through it while you're talking.

If you have time, try to get your audience involved. Ask them questions, and encourage them to ask questions in turn. When you're ready to wrap up your speech, summarize your key points and supporting data and tie them together in your conclusion. The chances are that your last comments are the ones your listeners will remember the longest, so end things with a bang and not a whimper.

Good speaking skills are essential in any type of job or work situation; whether you're asking your boss for a raise or debating an issue at a union meeting, or even criticizing a subordinate's performance, you must be able to get your message across—clearly. Several good books are available that can give you further guidance (see bibliography), but the only real way to become a good speaker is to practice. Join a local women's group or professional organization—offer to give a presentation. Volunteer to talk to a local high school class about careers in your field, or any interesting hobbies you may have. The more experience you get, the more comfortable—and vocal—you'll be.

Listen Up!

> A good listener is not only popular everywhere, but after a while [s]he gets to know something.
> WILSON MIZNER

Do you ever have one of those days when you feel like screaming, "Isn't anyone listening to me?" People may be *hearing* what you're saying, but they're not really *listening*. You may as well be talking to a brick wall—an awful feeling.

However, let's turn the tables around for a minute. How good a listener are *you?* Ask yourself the following questions:

- Do I sometimes finish a person's sentence for him/her because I'm eager to demonstrate that I really understand what's being said?

- Am I busy thinking up counterarguments while someone is talking to me?

- Does the urge to convey my own message lead me to begin another sentence or idea before someone else has finished her/his own?

- Do I "tune out" when I think I already know what someone is going to say to me?

- Do I tend to draw conclusions before listening to someone's entire message?

- Do I concentrate on just the "text" of someone's message and ignore the accompanying nonverbal signals?

- Does my face say "Yes I'm listening" while my mind daydreams about a vacation in the South Pacific?

If you answered "yes" to any one of these questions (and most of us will), your listening habits can stand some improvement.

Listening is not a skill that comes naturally to most people. Maybe it's because we're all suffering from information overload. All day long we are bombarded by all kinds of messages—from television, radio, friends, bosses, co-workers, and families—not to mention the noise pollution we also encounter. It's no wonder that people sometimes "turn off"—probably to keep themselves from short-circuiting!

Perhaps bad listening habits are symptoms of what journalist Tom Wolfe calls the "Me Decade"—the shift from the 60s' concern with social welfare to the 70s' emphasis on one's own personal welfare. Real listening requires that you submerge your own ego (or opinions) temporarily and concentrate on someone else's feelings or point of view.

Listening can become more enjoyable if you don't regard it as a time-consuming nuisance, but consider it an opportunity to gather more information about the world and people around you. Good listening skills are very important at work. How well you listen to your boss and coworkers will determine your own responses to them. If you're a bad listener, you take the risk of responding incorrectly, and you can come away with very different messages from the ones intended. This in turn can lead to additional misunderstandings, mistakes, and bad working relationships. It can also mean the difference between a job poorly done and a job well done.

Becoming a good listener requires practice. Here are some tips to help you get an earful:

- Try to put yourself in the other person's shoes. Why is she/he delivering this particular message? Suspend your own beliefs for the moment and concentrate on the other person's point of view.

- Listen to others with an open mind. Try not to enter any dialogue with preconceived notions of what the other person will say. Your certainty can lead you to hear the "wrong" message. Also, don't be so busy concocting a rebuttal that you tune out the message altogether.

- Don't be so anxious to state your own case that you interrupt someone else or end up finishing their statements. Swallow the urge to put in your two cents' worth before someone else has finished. (Hold your breath if you have to!)

- Learn to read the nonverbal cues put out by people. Do the medium and the message coincide? Someone may be saying, "No, I don't mind doing this extra report," while his or her eyes are throwing poison darts at you.

- Watch your own body language. Your mind may be listening, but if your hands are playing with your hair, or you keep looking at your watch, or examining your fingernails, the message you're giving is: "I'm not interested." Relax, look the speaker in the eye, and keep your hands and feet still. An occasional smile, nod, or an "I see" or "I understand," can put the other person at ease and demonstrate that you are paying attention. And since you can't talk and listen at the same time, keep quiet.

Concentrate on improving your own listening skills so that, with practice, you can eliminate bad habits. Good listening requires conscious effort on your part. So come on—lend an ear!

Meeting Time

When I first started working, I really *dreaded* attending departmental meetings. There I was, surrounded by all these whiz kids who were coming up with eighty brilliant ideas per minute. I was so intimidated I couldn't even think straight. It took me a long time to realize that everyone's ideas weren't always brilliant and that my contributions were just as valuable *or* open to criticism. Now that I've gotten to know my coworkers better and have opened my mouth a few times, I'm beginning to feel much more comfortable. I'm actually beginning to enjoy these meetings!
— A WORKING WOMAN

You are back at your desk, revived and relaxed, basking in the comfort of your own private space. Somehow you made it through the meeting. But if you left that meeting wishing you'd had the courage to voice your idea or contribute a comment or two, perhaps you didn't really get through it after all. And if someone came up with a similar idea, and was credited with it simply because he or she had the gumption to speak up while you sat wondering how and when to present yourself, where does that leave you? Anonymous.

Business meetings are a means of communication. Some meetings—for example, regularly scheduled staff meetings—are held to keep employees abreast of what's happening in an organization. Other meetings are scheduled to discuss specific issues, or maybe come up with some new project ideas, or kick around a tough problem and get some staff input on possible solutions.

A meeting can be a good source of exposure—a chance for you to show your coworkers, boss, and even your boss's boss what you are made of. But some first-jobbers, faced with this unfamiliar situation, believe they can best preserve their "dignity" by doing a slow, graceful fadeout into the background. They'll think to themselves: "If I just keep my mouth shut, I won't be able to put my foot in it."

Well there *are* several ways to make yourself look bad at a meeting—and hiding yourself away in some cozy little corner is one way. Keeping your mouth shut will only "lock in" any valuable contributions you may be able to offer.

The best way to look good at a meeting is to avoid looking bad. How? Don't slouch in the corner staring at your hands. Be positive. Relax. You're on the inside now, where you can learn from others and where others can learn from you. Feel good about being there, and remember: you *are* there because you're an asset to your department and your company.

Ideally, those attending a meeting should be given

advance notice of the agenda so that they then have a chance to consider the topics and formulate some ideas. Sometimes, however, you'll find yourself participating in a meeting with no advance warning, in which case you'll just have to "wing it" and think on your feet. At any rate, before any meeting, at least try to find out who will be present and the objectives of the meeting. The better prepared you are, the more confident you'll feel.

Here are some tips to help you participate in business meetings with more confidence:

- If the seating order is not prearranged, don't linger on the outskirts of the group or surround yourself with a "protective" layer of friends. Take a seat near the "big shots." You might be a "big shot" yourself someday.

- Don't be afraid to be the first one to speak. When you want to make a comment or ask a question, do it early in the meeting. The more you hesitate, the more nervous you'll become. And the more nervous you are, the more you will feel that what you finally say will have to sound profound.

- Speaking of profound—don't make a speech. Remember that guy in Psychology I who dominated each class with at least a dozen deeply meaningful but totally irrelevant tales? He was digging for words and speaking only to hear the sound of his own voice. No one needed it then, and no one needs it now. Your comments should always be succinct and relevant to the topic. Use simple, direct language. Support your points with facts and not abstract statements. (It helps to formulate your questions or comments in your own mind before attempting to impress them on others. You can jot down key points *before* you speak to help you remember.)

• Speak slowly and in a tone of voice that will enable everyone in the room to hear you. Avoid speaking in a monotone, because it will lead others to believe that you are: (1) boring, (2) uninterested, or (3) a student of Howard Cosell.

• Don't be self-effacing. Leading off your comment by saying "I may be wrong, but—" or "One small point . . ." will detract from the value of your statement. Be proud of your position. Don't appease any male chauvinists in the group by trying to appear more feminine (and therefore, less "threatening"). Giggling, fidgeting, and blushing are indirect ways of apologizing for being who and what you are, and unless you trip and fall into someone's lap, there's no need to apologize.

• Never say never. Don't be so consumed by your own thoughts or ideas that you are not open to discussion. Bend a little. Be prepared to reason, not argue. If a proposed idea seems bad, don't be too critical of it; suggest a different approach instead. Support another viewpoint by phrasing it so that it seems like an extension of (or variation on) the first idea. For instance, "That's a valid point, but maybe we should also consider . . ." or "I like that idea, but let's look at it from this other angle. . . ."

• If you are referring to something that was said earlier in the meeting, try to rephrase what was said, to clarify its relationship to your own comments.

Just as there are ways to avoid making yourself look bad, there are ways to prevent others from making you look bad. Beware of those who will try to steal your ideas. Statements like "That's a good idea—I'll work out the details and put it into action for you," are bad news. Such remarks are a good indication that someone is about to take your idea and make it his/hers. Respond immediately. Tell the person that you've got something specific in mind, or that you've thought it all out and know exactly how *you* are going to handle it.

Those who aren't interested in stealing your idea may be interested in attacking it. The first thing is to remain calm, because to overreact is to have others believe that their criticisms are valid. Again, be positive. And think ahead. Imagine yourself coming out of it as the winner. Reason with those who challenge you; start by saying something like: "You have a point, but you missed some important facts. You might change your mind, once you can see the entire picture." By doing so, you will make it seem that those who challenged you have not been as thorough as you. And once you've got them playing in your ball park, the odds are in your favor.

Business Etiquette

> Those that are good manners at the court are as ridiculous in the country, as the behavior of the country is most mockable at the court.
>
> WILLIAM SHAKESPEARE,
> *As You Like It*

Welcome to the "court"—the business world. Perhaps you instinctively rebel against the idea of "stepping into character" to comply with the conventional modes of behavior so typical of the business environment. Relax. You won't have to alter dramatically the "real you." But the way in which you present yourself to others *is* important to your career. You will have to create a professional image.

The way you relate to your business colleagues is an essential part of that image. In these professional relationships the "rules" of business etiquette apply.

In the past we could rely on such stalwart defenders of correct behavior as Emily Post to tell us when we should wear our white gloves or when we could eat with our fingers. But even Emily would be at a loss to tell us how to take a male client out to lunch without stepping on his ego and/or blowing the business relationship. Business etiquette is harder to quantify because professional behavior is more the result of common sense than of a strict code of conduct. Professionalism cannot be taught, but it can be learned (alas, often in the school of hard knocks). If there is a general principle to follow, it's that you should treat your colleagues—male or female—with confidence, courtesy, and respect.

Keep in mind that the rules of business etiquette depend on the business relationship of the people involved (e.g., buyer to seller, boss to employee, etc.), and not on the age or sex of the participants. As a professional, you should expect to be treated as an equal, and you owe it to yourself to see that you are not disappointed. But remember that most men were taught, at some point in their lives, that women should be given the kid-glove treatment whenever possible. Older men, in particular, have lived by that rule. As more women enter the job market, a few of the younger males, by inclination or force (or maybe gentle persuasion), have had their consciousnesses raised to a level where they are wary of patronizing attitudes. But a few diehards still linger back in never-never land, behaving as if chivalry were some kind of male hormone they have no control over. They believe that they should be "perfect gentlemen" at all times, particularly when they are interacting with women.

Until recently, the business environment was one that supported this view. Today the situation has improved to some extent. Be patient. If a male colleague insists on opening the door for you and hailing the cab as you leave the office, his actions should not become the target of undue bitterness or cries of "Male chauvinist pig!" In most cases a gentle reminder that you're self-reliant will do it. You've come a long way, but there's still a long way to travel and it's best to remember that a good balance of diplomacy and self-respect will make the going a lot smoother.

Following are some general guidelines of business etiquette.

Courtesy Titles

- If you are married, you can keep your maiden name if you want to.

- You can use "Ms." for business purposes regardless of your marital status.

- Do not use courtesy title (Ms., Miss, Mrs.) with your signature; use only your name. (The title "Dr." is optional on your business card.)

- When you receive a letter or telephone call from a female associate, make a note of whether she uses a courtesy title and address her as such. (Some women are still offended by the use of "Ms." so make every effort to establish preference.)

Telephone Manners

- Answer your telephone immediately and state your name.

- Let the person who made the call end it. If you are in a rush, you can take the initiative and end it yourself.

- When you telephone an associate, tell his or her secretary your name and title and the reason for your call.

- When you call someone, start off by asking whether he or she has time to talk. Don't ask "Do you have a minute?" unless you really mean *one* minute. Specify the approximate amount of time you'll need. When necessary, offer to call later.

Introductions

- Stand up and shake hands when greeting a business associate or visitor, regardless of his or her age, sex, or status. Since some men are uncertain about shaking a woman's hand, make the first move to avoid any awkwardness.

- When you arrive at someone else's office for an appointment, tell the secretary or receptionist your name, the person you are calling on, and the time of your appointment.

- When you are introducing others, give the name of the highest-ranking person first. For instance: "Ben Jones [your boss], this is Mary Gray [your colleague]."

- When a visitor enters your office, stand and indicate where he or she is to be seated. Rise again when the caller starts to leave, and show him or her to the door.

Who Goes First

- When you are walking in a group, let your superiors or any visitors lead the way.

- Let your boss precede you through an open door. If you happen to be leading, hold the door open for your boss, and for other higher-ranking associates.

- In all other situations (where status is irrelevant) the first person to reach the door opens it and holds it for the other. (You may find that some men will make a mad dash to the door so they can hold it for you. Grin and bear it.)

Common Sense

- We can all put on our own coats, one hopes. However, if you are a hapless victim of the "elusive sleeve syndrome," do allow someone to be of service. And be ready to return the favor.

- Times have changed. Make every attempt to leave the elevator as though it were an elevator and not a sinking ship. Those nearest the door, whether male or female, get off first. Those toward the rear leave last. Again, some men still believe in "women and children first." If you find that five men are all standing around waiting for you to exit, do so by all means—before the elevator sinks!

Miracle on 34th Street—or Main Street

- If you're fortunate enough to spot an empty taxi, don't hesitate to flag it down. The first person to witness this miracle should act immediately. You wouldn't want this precious commodity to pass you by.

The "Dating" Game

- Don't allow yourself to be treated as a "date" when you dine out with a male coworker or business acquaintance. You're eating for business, not pleasure. Accept responsibility for your share of the bill; be adamant about this if necessary.

- If the occasion is expressly for business, the person who instigated the appointment is generally the one whose company is paying. In other cases, if both parties agree, you can alternate in paying the check. To avoid hesitation or embarrassments, these arrangements should be made *in advance.*

HELP FOR THE TONGUE- AND PEN-TIED

There are many books and pamphlets that can help you become a better communicator. Here are a few useful ones:

Writing as a Professional Activity is a booklet that offers sound advice for writing, both on and off the job. Topics covered include: the stages of writing, developing outlines, writing drafts, and developing your writing style. It is available for $2.50 from:

The National Association for Women Deans,
Administrators, and Counselors
1028 Connecticut Avenue, NW
Washington, D.C. 10036

One of the best writing aids around is *The Elements of Style* (third edition) by William Strunk, Jr., and E. B. White. This invaluable little book is the bible for correct and concise writing and should be mandatory reading for everyone who has to write or loves to write. It covers all elementary rules of usage and principles of composition. The section covering style is itself a lesson in clear, lucid writing. The book is available for $1.95 in most bookstores, or write:

Macmillan Publishing Company, Inc.
866 Third Avenue
New York, N.Y. 10022

The three following publications are all excellent guides to nonsexist communication:

Guidelines for Equal Treatment of the Sexes by the McGraw-Hill Book Company Division of McGraw-Hill Publishing is available free from:

McGraw-Hill
Public Affairs Department
Room 369
1221 Avenue of the Americas
New York, N.Y. 10020

Without Bias: A Guidebook for Nondiscriminatory Communication is available for $4.00 from:

The International Association of
Business Communicators
870 Market Street, Suite 928
San Francisco, Cal. 94102

The Sensitive Listener of the 1980's: A Glossary of Terms is available from:

The American Federation of Television and
Radio Artists
National Women's Division
Box 23013
Minneapolis, Minn. 55423

ADVICE FOR THE SHY, THE MEEK, AND THE INTIMIDATED

"No one else in my family is shy, but I've been shy since childhood. My parents knew shyness wasn't a 'virtue'; still, they used it to explain my behavior whenever I became uncomfortable in the presence of others. 'She's just quiet,' they would say. Since I was *always* uncomfortable around strangers, I learned to use shyness as a defense. It was a problem then, and it's a problem now. There are times when I'm proud of my accomplishments and capabilities. I tell myself that I'm 'okay,' and I really do believe it. The problem is, few people will ever know it because I'm too shy to blow my own horn."

Shyness. It's a common problem. According to Dr. Philip G. Zimbardo, author of *Shyness: What It Is and What to Do About It,* four out of every ten people you meet—an estimated 84 million Americans—deem themselves shy at least part of the time.

Shyness is often equated with modesty or femininity. Many people view shyness as a positive trait, a virtue. But most shy people—like the first-jobber who analyzed her problem above—realize that shyness affects their lives in ways that are anything but positive. Shyness in any form is a handicap, and although we may not always be aware of it, the effects of shyness can be paralyzing.

Shyness is a barrier to good communication. It can prevent you from effectively expressing yourself, speaking up for your rights, or even offering your own opinions. Shyness can make you overly self-conscious about the way you look, sound—or work. And shyness can affect the ways you are evaluated by others, including your boss and coworkers.

Since shy people often have trouble communicating their good qualities or aspirations, they may not get the advice or recognition they deserve. In most group settings—including the work world—the chosen leaders are those who can demonstrate their skills and talents to others, those who can show they have something valuable to offer. Those twenty good ideas floating around in your head won't matter if no one else ever gets to know about them. That annual report you worked so hard to collect data for won't add to your achievement record if no one else is aware of your contributions. Behind-the-scenes workers generally remain behind the scenes. Shyness can keep a good person down and can be a real impediment to advancement.

Fortunately, shyness is "curable." Shyness can be something you "grow out of" as you have more opportunities to interact with others and to practice simple social skills. Even if you never totally overcome shyness, you *can* learn to control it. (Did you know that Eleanor Roosevelt, Barbara Walters, and Carol Burnett have all been self-proclaimed shys?)

The key to overcoming shyness is training. Don't be concerned with creating a "new you"; you don't need to be reborn to overcome shyness. What you must do is simply to learn to pinpoint those situations likely to bring on an "attack" of shyness. Then act to change your behavior when necessary.

For example, suppose you're particularly shy about talking to "strangers." Well, start to change your behavior in small ways. Begin with the kinds of situations that threaten you least. Say hello to a few new people this week. When the greeting becomes a matter of habit, expand on it—try complimenting others on their shoes, their haircuts; follow through on their responses. ("Where do you do your shopping?" "Where do you have your hair cut?") Ask for advice; express interest in other people. ("How did you get your job? Do you enjoy your work?")

If you get tongue-tied during conversations, try rehearsing a few openers, follow-up statements, and questions. One Catalyst editor who calls herself a "fellow shy" offers the following advice:

> Focus on what it is you're talking about. Concentrate—be involved in the conversation—and you won't have as much time or energy to worry about yourself. Also, don't demand of yourself that you have to be 100 percent articulate, accurate, witty, and profound every time you open your mouth. *No* one ever is. And remember—the person you are speaking to may also be one of those four out of ten shys! Look to them for clues and try to help *them* relax and feel comfortable with *you.*

It's a good idea to ask your friends if they've had problems with shyness and what has helped them to overcome it. For instance, one first-jobber we talked to was shy about speaking to clients over the phone. She found it very helpful to jot down a brief summary of the points she wanted to cover and then, "just take a very deep breath and let your fingers do the dialing! Once I got the ball rolling, I forgot about my shyness and got down to the business at hand."

In time and with increased familiarity, your interactions and conversations with others will become a natural and efficient means of communication. It is possible that the "basically shy" person you once were will still be there, sometimes. The important thing, however, is that you will have gained enough control over your shyness to increase your self-confidence and to further your chances of advancement. Remember, as Goethe said, "It is equally a mistake to hold one's self too high, or to rate one's self too cheap." So don't let shyness keep *you* down!

STRATEGY SESSION

10

Now THAT YOU KNOW the skills that should put you on the road to advancement, use some strategy to make sure you reach your destination.

Strategy, it seems, has gotten a bad reputation of late. Maybe it's because of Watergate and those who brought this country's political situation tumbling down. Thanks to them, strategy now smacks of dirty politics, back-stabbing, and everything vile and detestable.

The tarnished image of strategy is highly unfortunate. Strategy doesn't involve compiling an "enemies list" or killing off your competition one by one. It can be clean, healthy, sometimes even fun. And without even knowing it, you are probably an old pro when it comes to strategy.

To use the Monopoly analogy again, remember how you and your brother would play and you'd always win by buying all the utilities and the railroads? You'd pass up hot-shot properties like Boardwalk and Park Place (which he always grabbed) because you noticed nobody ever landed on them anyway. That was strategy, my friend.

Remember how you had a crush on that guy in your history class and the only way you could attract his attention was by moving your chair closer and closer to his? And when he did notice you (how couldn't he—when you were practically breathing down his neck?) you'd nonchalantly turn your head away? You were using not one but two strategies then (the second one fondly known as "playing hard to get"). You were quite the strategist!

Well, the stakes have changed now. You're no longer playing for hotels on Marvin Gardens or vying for the class heart-throb. What you're after is a promotion, the next step up your career ladder. But the playing of the game hasn't changed—you still need a little strategy to come out a winner.

Networking Isn't Just on Television

In the last few years a new word has sprung into our midst—"networking." But it has nothing to do with the ratings war the three major networks wage every season. Rather the term "networking," as it's used in the business world, refers to people setting up professional relationships. These relationships can exist among employees in a company, as well as among individuals in various companies. The purpose, though, is the same: networking provides workers with information not ordinarily available through regular channels, offers career help and advice, and functions as a support system.

Networking is not a new strategy. It has always been part of the business world. But networking has gotten more attention lately because of the growth of exclusively female networks within companies. Taken as a whole, these networks are seen as a greater "new-girl network" that has arisen to rival the traditional "old-boy network." Why the need for a new-girl network? As women started entering the work world in great numbers, many of them soon made their way into the ranks of management. There they suddenly found themselves locked out of a lot of important business discussions. It seems that much of the give and take of ideas between men in management occurs in many informal settings—at a bar after work, in the men's room during work hours, in the locker room at the tennis club—from which women were either tacitly or legally excluded. Short of storming down the door to the men's room, women soon realized that the only alternative was to form their own buddy systems, their own information networks.

What can joining the woman's network at your company do for you? Many things. Moral support is one commodity that a network offers. As one woman manager explained: "The network lets us know who our friends are, whom we can turn to if we have a problem." If you're like most women starting out, you probably have a tendency to think that the mistakes you've made or the problems you've encountered are yours alone. Reaching out to other women in your company, talking to them about your problems, and discovering that your experiences have been shared by countless others can give you that extra boost of reassurance you need.

And most important, joining a woman's network will supply you with firsthand information about job openings in your company. Thus you will be able to apply for openings before they are posted on the bulletin board in Personnel, or before your boss tells you.

And through your network, you'll learn the real truth about working for Mr. Dithers, which may save you the unfortunate step of applying for a position only to discover a few months later that you and Mr. Dithers were not meant to be a team. As Susan Dresner, formerly of McGraw-Hill, points out, "A network functions much the same way kids in college share notes on a professor. Only now it's notes on a boss you're comparing." Taking that metaphor a little further, remember how those friends in college also passed along hints on how to get good marks in a professor's class? Though you're not after A's anymore, you could use advice on what to say to a potential boss during an interview, also tips on getting along with him or her once you've been hired into that new position. Trust the members of your network to pass that information on to you.

If networks are so helpful, why is it that not every company has one? Like yours, for instance? It may very well be that your company has one after all; search a little harder. Many networks have been forced to go "underground" due to company hostility. In the words of Ted Scott of Bankers Trust in New York, "You have to realize that any management is sensitive about the formation of employee coalitions, no matter who's doing it. They don't want anything to dilute their sense of control." And to many companies, an all-female network might seem especially threatening: headstrong females scheming to topple the male hierarchy.

Aside from male corporate heads, a lot of women themselves aren't exactly sold on women networks. And it's not that these women are suffering from the "queen bee syndrome" and refuse to work hand in hand with other women in their company. One computer programmer we talked to explained it this way: "I have found it most helpful not to see myself apart from the men in my company. I think women do themselves a great disservice if they form splinter groups within an organization. I have to presume that I can learn from the men and associate on an equal level with them. They might think I don't have the right to, but I go ahead and do so anyway. And the doing is the learning."

Maybe this woman's words make a lot of sense to you. If you're in a job situation in which you're working closely with men, you might feel that openly joining a women's network can work to your disadvantage, casting a pall of suspicion and distrust upon you. But think of the benefits of joining that network; they just might outweigh the risks. You'll be able to find out how other women handle their problems with male coworkers, and you can use them as a sounding board to any strategies you've devised in dealing with the men in your work life. And it is probably only through your network that you can get hold of important information your male colleagues may be keeping from you.

Aside from joining a network within your company, it's also vital that you start making professional contacts with people in your field. Join a professional organization, attend trade shows, conventions, seminars, press conferences. Be wherever you can meet people in your sphere of work. Not only will the contacts you make at these places keep you abreast of latest trends and information, they will also prove invaluable if you ever want to leave your company and need job leads. So start mingling with your associates. Print a batch of business cards, if you don't already have some, to hand out. Start a file of all those you collect from others.

And do "use" your contacts, or else you'll lose them. All that means is keeping in touch with them through an occasional phone call and a lunch now and then to "touch base." If you keep an ongoing rapport with your contacts, you won't feel hesitant about getting in touch with them when you do have a favor to ask. If you're in a jam at work, call a contact. Let's say your boss has asked you to track down a reasonably priced printer and you don't know where to begin, short of calling every printer in the phone book. But Debra, a woman you met at a recent seminar, does a lot of work with printers and can supply you with the answer you need. In return, she may call you one day to ask about any openings in your company or about something you can help her with on her job.

As you rise higher in your career, you'll be in a better position for paying back favors than you are now. But it doesn't hurt to get in the habit of offering your services, any job leads you know of, and whatever else you may have at your disposal.

That John Donne line "No man is an island" is especially true in the work world. You won't rise like a meteor without the help of a few friends. By networking, both in and out of your company, you'll be assured of having all the help you need.

Much Ado About Mentors

To put it simply, you can't get ahead in business without a little help from some friends. The people in your various networks will be one circle of friends to help you. In addition, you should be on the lookout for a mentor, preferably one within your own company. A mentor is a person who will function as a role model for you, someone who will take a direct interest in your career and who will help you learn the proverbial ropes. Most of all, a mentor will ensure that you get the visibility you need in your company in order to get ahead.

Like networking, mentoring is not a new concept. Mentor–protégé relationships have always been found through the ages, especially in the arts, athletics, philosophy, and education. In fact, the word "mentor" comes to us from the Greek poet Homer. Mentor was the friend and adviser of Odysseus in the Greek epics. (Actually, those of you who remember your Greek mythology know that Mentor was really Athena in disguise—the original female role model!)

Mentors you have had so far probably have been your teachers: that fifth-grade teacher who spotted your talent in music and persuaded you to take music lessons, or the college professor who spent extra time critiquing your poetry, because she felt you showed promise as a poet. By offering you their knowledge and experience, and exhibiting confidence in you, these early mentors helped lend a sense of direction to your life and tried their darnedest to help you get there.

A business mentor will do the same for you, making you career-conscious and goal-oriented. The sooner you enlist the help of a mentor (or mentors), the sooner your goals can be reached. As you know, you're competing with many other candidates right in your own company, all vying to get ahead. Having a mentor guarantees that you won't get lost in the shuffle. And if you're one of a minority of women in a male-dominated company, your mentor can help you gain the professional legitimacy you may feel you lack. That's what a mentor did for Aurora Rubin, a manager at a large national accounting firm: "My mentor made sure that I got on 'good' accounting jobs; by that I mean visible jobs where I had some in-charge responsibilities and where I could learn. So that after I had been on the job for a while and somebody requested a 'good' accountant, I could always point out my experience, versus being 'lost in the mill.'"

How do you find a mentor? For Aurora, the task was simple enough: her mentor found her. "This 'godfather' of mine had a habit of looking through the files of new-comers," she explains, "and he'd try to get anyone who interested him for one reason or another on his job. He was impressed with the fact that I was a woman trying to make it in a field that was virtually all male at the time."

Aurora's case is really the exception to the rule. Along with job-hunting and apartment-hunting, plan on going mentor-hunting too. Where to begin? Barbara Holt, a leading management and career consultant, advises: "Learn the formal and informal organizational structure of your company to find out the power spheres. Then think of where you want to be next, which means thinking about your skills and where they fit. Then look to see who has the most influence and control in that power sphere you see yourself heading toward."

You may find a whole slew of likely mentors within that power sphere. Who's the right one for you? Kate Harrigan, a corporate executive, suggests that you approach an individual whose personality is similar to yours: "If you're an assertive, aggressive kind of person, look for someone who's even more so than you. If you're a cautious person that sits and watches, look for someone who always sits in the back and watches what goes on, then make a value judgment."

Can your boss be your mentor? After all, much of what a mentor does for you—sees that you're visible to the higher-ups in your corporation, takes an active interest in your career, encourages you to move ahead—is ideally ascribed to a boss. Most of the professionals we spoke to said they have seen numerous successful working relationships in which the boss was also the mentor. But, these professionals point out, it is very significant that in all these relationships the boss was very interested and eager to assume that second role, very often extending the offer of mentorship to the subordinate. Their final warning to you on this whole matter: don't try to force your boss into becoming your mentor if the willingness isn't there. It may be that your boss feels uneasy singling you out as his or her protégé over your coworkers. Or perhaps your career ambitions conflict with your boss's. Whatever the reason, if you sense reluctance on the part of your boss, search for your mentor in the ranks of higher management or in another department.

What should you beware of in your relationship with your mentor? Try not to treat your mentor like a god, advises one executive recruiter: "Be critical of him or her. Don't take everything your mentor says as gospel. And learn from your mentor's mistakes too." This keep-an-open-mind philosophy is also advocated by Kate Harrigan, a mentor to a young trainee at her company: "I tell my trainee, 'Don't let me influence you so much. Because then you'll wind up getting tunnel vision. Just take what I tell you and sort it out by yourself!'"

Also be wary that your mentor doesn't try to protect you

from the harsh realities of the work world (for example, political squabbles). This trap often befalls women who have male mentors. Some men may regard the mentor–protégé relationship as akin to the father–daughter relationship and like good fathers they may go out of their way to shield their "daughters" from all things distasteful. If you feel your mentor is creating a cloistered environment in your company for you, let him (or her) know that you want to face the work-world realities. Tell your mentor that although you know his intentions are good, the more "bad experiences" you're exposed to, and with his help survive, the better equipped you'll be in your career.

Once you reap the rewards of your relationship with your mentor and are in a position to be a mentor yourself, by all means do take on that role and help others. A recent *Harvard Business Review* study shows that executives who have had a mentor earn more money at a younger age, are more likely to follow a career plan, and have sponsored more protégés than executives who never had a mentor. So when you're ready, willing, and able, extend a hand to some person on her first job who shows a lot of promise but is just a bit green in the ways of the business world—as you were once.

It's a Man's World: Working with Men

It's funny how much faith we place in change, or at least in the belief that everyone is affected by certain events as strongly as we are. Take the women's movement, for example. You know how the movement altered your perception of yourself as a woman; it only stands to reason that the lives of countless other women were similarly influenced. And the men . . . the women's movement turned them into a new species, you say, freed them of their macho hang-ups, allowed them finally to relate to women as equals.

Well, it's hard to guess just what effect the women's movement has had on men, but from talking to some women and hearing how men treat them at work, it sometimes seems as if there has been little effect. In the work world, some things have stayed as they always have been. To show you that sometimes the more things change the more they stay the same, here's just a sampling of testimonials from some of those women:

"I was part of a predominantly female staff. My boss would refer to us (always in front of visitors he'd want to impress) as his 'harem.'"

"I was on an out-of-town assignment with two male coworkers. One night, one of them started banging on my hotel door. I let him in to see what was the matter. It soon became obvious that what he had on his mind wasn't what I had on mine, and I showed him to the door. When we got back to headquarters, this guy filed a complaint against me, accusing me of trying to seduce him. I was severely reprimanded by my superior for supposedly playing the temptress."

"It always amazes me, in the high-ranking position I occupy, that every time I walk into a client's office with my assistant, a man, they always assume that I am his assistant."

And if you're still not convinced that the work world can still be a discriminatory environment, would you believe it if you heard a male executive say it's so? "Women have to work twice as hard as men," acknowledges Tom Robinson of the American Management Association. "They have two battles to fight—one, with their own ability to do the job, and two, with the subtle discrimination that exists, the extra barriers that are put up for them to jump."

Women who are members of predominantly male staffs often face the toughest barriers. "I have had problems on project teams where I was the *only* woman," remembers Angela Hamill, a senior staff person at a national management consulting firm. "At first, unless I was the project director, I found myself being eased out of the decision-making process; project meetings would be held and I wouldn't be notified. Once I heard a colleague explain to another, 'She's only here because we have to have a woman on the project.' He knew that wasn't true; my credentials were better than almost everybody else's. But I had to learn not to get too angry about things like that. But now that there are more women working here, there's always at least one other woman on a project team, and that makes a real difference."

For women working in nontraditional fields such as the skilled trades, the barriers are often more difficult to overcome. Dana Rosen, a journeyman carpenter in the Midwest, recalled some of the problems she had as an apprentice: "It's hard to explain what happened. It wasn't the obscene graffiti. That situation was much easier to handle. What got to me was that I was totally ignored. It was like feeling invisible. In all kinds of little ways they let me know I wasn't important; that my work wasn't important, didn't mean anything.

"It was very hard to take. There were all kinds of little hostile remarks; work was taken away from me; other people were given credit for my work. I was made to feel that I had been hired only because I was a woman.

"What happened was, I began to believe that myself. I would come home exhausted from the strain of trying to keep up my confidence in myself. It even affected relationships with my family. I finally got angry and I started to complain. But it wasn't until a local antidiscrimination agency filed suit that the construction company finally started to listen to me. The suit made things better for me. It didn't change everything, but enough was changed about the way I was treated so that I could continue.

"That kind of harassment is something women should know about and be on guard against—even outside the construction trades. You have to remember who you are and what you want. You have to stand up for your rights."

Whether it's subtle or blatant, some discrimination still exists. And you had better be prepared to deal with it. But don't be so eager as to hurl accusations of sexism at every male in sight at every opportunity. Don't think of your boss as a male chauvinist pig just because he comments on how nice you look. (Wouldn't you expect a woman to notice?) A lot of behavior that is seemingly sexist can be quite innocent in nature; very often it's an attempt by men to be polite or flattering. Don't allow yourself to be too sensitive; develop a tolerant attitude and a sense of perspective.

What do you do, though, when you do have a justified complaint? Let's say your boss, an older man, has a habit of calling all the women in the office "dear." At first it didn't bother you, but now that you're involved in high-powered meetings with your boss and several male colleagues, it's embarrassing when you're called "dear" in front of the men, many of whom you've heard snickering. You're aware that at these meetings your credibility is seriously undermined. How can you approach your boss about this?

First of all, give your boss the benefit of the doubt. In calling you "dear," your boss is not intentionally out to destroy you professionally; he just thinks that the pet name is complimentary, and the notion that it can be misconstrued as sexist has never crossed his mind. He may call all the women in his life "dear"—his wife, sisters, daughters. And it's true, the majority of men aren't aware when they're delivering sexist remarks. So enlighten your boss to the issue of sexism. The next time another "dear" pops out of his mouth when the two of you are alone (never in front of others), say "I really don't like being called 'dear.' You wouldn't call Tom or Doug that, and I feel it isn't professional. I know that you don't mean any harm by it, but I'd prefer not to be called by anything but my name or title in the office." It shouldn't take him long to realize that he has set up two sets of standards for treating (or at least addressing) the men and women working under him. He will appreciate your honesty (and understanding way of correcting him), probably thinking twice every time he gets the impulse to call you "dear" again.

There's been a lot of talk in recent years of just how effective the strategy of "acting like one of the boys" can be for women. Some critics say that in imitating the behavior of men, women only confirm the belief that men are superior. "Any group of people who have been told for a long time—for centuries, in fact—that they are inferior would have a tendency to try to measure up to the so-called 'superiors,'" says Dr. Jean Baker Miller, author of *Toward a New Psychology of Women,* in an article in *Working Woman.*

Then there are those who regard "acting like one of the boys" less a gesture of tipping your hat to your superiors and more in the vein of "When in Rome, do as the Romans do." According to Ted Scott, a personnel executive at Bankers Trust Company, "If you have good interpersonal skills and you can take a joke, and you can kid back, it's very disarming to men. You are in fact functioning like one of the boys. Your fit seems to be enhanced."

The only drawback to adopting the "one of the boys" strategy is that in doing so you're not giving yourself a chance to develop your own style, or to even show the men your real self. Jane Higgins, a woman on her first job, who works almost solely with men, admits: "The best way to handle the men on the job is to 'become one of the guys.' I feel I can't be myself around them. In many respects, they haven't seen my true person." And though Ted Scott recognizes the benefits of acting like one of the boys, he also believes you can go much further if you come to work exactly as you are: "Your greatest effectiveness is when you're bringing the most of yourself you can to any job situation, because that's when you're going to be sensed as somebody to be reckoned with."

Maybe it is easy for a man to say this. The pendulum does swing both ways for a man: he can be himself, and still be one of the boys; both options are open to him. It may not be so easy for women. Most women find they have to decide between the two at some point in their work lives. Jane Higgins, for example, was on an out-of-town business trip with some male colleagues and found herself taunted into going to an X-rated movie. "They turned to me and said, 'Are you going to behave like all the other women we've worked with, stay in your room all night like a scared cat?' I had no choice but to say, 'Sure, I'll go to the movies with you.' In the back of my mind, though, I was thinking, 'Should I do this? Is it going to get around the office that I went to an X-rated movie?' But it was damned if I did go, damned if I didn't. Luckily for me, the movie turned out to be rated R, not X, after all."

This incident indicates the realities of working with men. They often hold the upper hand—it's their game we're playing, their rules we're following. If we don't choose to act like one of the boys, then we must be on our very best behavior, avoiding the slightest possibility of tripping up. Because if we do fail, we feel that the men out there will disenfranchise an entire legion of working women on the actions of one. It is a heavy burden, also an unfair one, that is carried by every working woman. And this burden does take its toll. "I ask myself, why can't I just go in there and be like everyone else, and not feel as if I'm on display and have to mind my P's and Q's all the time," grumbles one woman on her first job. "But I feel I do. And this takes a certain percentage out of you by the end of the week."

Such is the state of the relations between men and women in the work world. Perhaps you're toiling away in a nonsexist atmosphere, where the men on the job treat you with the professional respect you deserve. But there's no telling when you might encounter sexism. It may crop up on your first job, or your second, third, or tenth job. Be prepared. It's a work-world reality for now, but one that you can learn to cope with if you are patient and understanding but also honest and firm.

The Bread-and-Butter Issue

Just about every working person, it seems, could stand a raise. And if you've just started working and are making a salary you can barely live on, let alone live on in the grand style to which you've become accustomed, a raise right now would seem like manna from heaven.

But raises aren't heaven-sent. Nor are they parceled out to employees who actually need more money (for example, to those who can't pay the rent and are sick of eating tuna fish every night). You can't depend on their coming with any regularity either (the exceptions to this, of course, are companies that have salary-review systems, or cases in which unions mandate cost-of-living increases). Most raises are "merit" raises and are meted out for achievement. Every time you get one, you'll know that's a sign from management that they're pleased with your performance. Thus raises can help give you a sense of your professional self-worth.

But there's nothing stopping you from *asking for* a raise, especially if you feel you've been doing a grade-A job and there's been no compensation for it. Even if you're on the first few months of your first job, don't feel it's presumptuous of you to ask for a raise. Don't be embarrassed either. Marsha Donovan, a woman on her first job, explains the attitude about salaries and raises shared by most first-jobbers: "When you just start working you have this student mentality, this belief that your low salary is justified; you're meant to live in a shambles for a while. But then one day you wake up and you realize you're worth more than you're getting paid. This happened to me after four months on the job. I asked for a raise at that time, and I got it."

How do you talk dollars and cents with your boss? First, gather your ammunition; you'll have to be able to convince your employer that you're worth a raise. Compile a list of your contributions to the company from the time you were hired or received your last raise. This step should be a relatively easy one for you if you've been keeping a career folder in which you note down your job accomplishments or ways you've expanded or improved your job as they happen. But if you haven't been keeping tabs, think back. Did you assume any new responsibilities? Eliminate time-consuming office procedures? The answers you come up with will serve as your bargaining tools.

Be prepared to walk into your boss's office with a definite dollar figure in mind. You may want to ask several of your coworkers or people in your network what typical raises are like in your company. If you're still unsure of how much to ask for, one figure most employers can live with is 15 percent (that's 15 percent of your yearly salary; a raise of $1,800 if you're earning $12,000).

Choose the right time to hold your bargaining session. You'll have a better chance of getting that raise if your company is in a good financial state. If it's in a particularly bad slump, you may want to hold off talking money for a while. And you might wait for an occasion when you're doing exceptionally well. The period after you've completed a successful project that's still fresh in your boss's mind couldn't be a better time. Also, don't approach your boss during a hectic period at work; wait till the storm dies down.

Another strategy that may increase your chances of getting a raise is to give your boss advance notice of your planned big event. All it takes is a memo saying you feel you deserve a raise due to your contributions to the company (list them), and would like to arrange a time to talk about the matter. That way it won't seem as if you're dropping your request for a raise like a bomb in your boss's lap. And you'll be giving your boss sufficient time to warm up to the idea of your getting a raise before you meet.

When you do see him/her, handle yourself in a businesslike manner. Present your case calmly. Don't raise your voice, and don't let a nervous quiver squeak through either (if you're nervous, a few deep breaths may help). Reiterate the reasons you feel you deserve a raise. If you sense your boss isn't particularly won over by your arguments, don't get angry. Declaring that "either I get this raise or I'm quitting" is not an effective bargaining tool. Issuing an ultimatum is an effective way to lose a job.

When that raise you asked for does appear in your pay envelope, thank your boss for it, even if you feel it's been long overdue. A little gratitude can go a long way. And if the raise you want is denied you, don't walk around fuming. That's not professional conduct. Your boss might begin to worry that you'll be less productive on account of your bitterness. So reassure your boss that you'll continue working as diligently as before. This behavior can only put you in good standing when raise-time rolls around again.

Secretaries: Out of the Secretarial Slot

It was a tight job market you encountered on leaving college, and the only positions offered were secretarial. Or you were lured by a fancy "assistant" title, or promised at the interview that you'd move up into the professional ranks within a month or two. Regardless of how you got there, stop bemoaning your fate. Life as a secretary needn't seem a bleak, dead-end trap. If you start developing your position, expanding it all you can (and there *are* distinct advantages to being a secretary), you can be on your way to a more satisfactory job before long.

First, get yourself in the right frame of mind. Don't belittle your position. Stop complaining that you know more than the idiot whose letters you have to type (and rewrite), or griping to everyone in earshot that your work is "beneath you." If you're a secretary in a company and field you're interested in, view your job as an all-important stepping stone to where you want to go. That's the attitude Ginny Mokarry, a recent college graduate, has about her secretarial position: "I got out of school expecting to land a job as a radio news writer. But then this offer to be a secretary at a major network came my way, and I couldn't pass it up. It's so hard to break into a network that it pays to get your foot in the door somehow."

It also helps to regard your job as a learning experience, sort of an advanced business seminar. Read, read, read everything you can lay your hands on—from the letters you type to the morning mail to interoffice memos to annual reports and back files. You may never again have access to so many business communications; take advantage of this situation. You'll get to learn your company's policies and operations, and how your boss and your department fit into the scheme of things. Then to fill in the blanks of your on-the-job education, ask questions of your boss and his or her colleagues. The more you learn, the more valuable you become, and hence the more likely to move ahead. And by asking questions you'll be sending a message across to your boss: "I'm not content to stay in this position indefinitely, I have higher aspirations."

The next thing for you to do is to spell out those aspirations to your boss. Have a chat with your boss and let him or her know you don't intend to stay a secretary for your entire career life, and would appreciate hearing of any management openings that do come up. And ask your boss for advice on how to get those positions. As Kathleen

Conway of New York Life Insurance notes, "You don't really get anywhere unless you ask for things, unless you say, 'Gee, I'd like to get the next job—what can I do to get it?"

To climb out of the secretarial niche, it's wise to jump at the chance to take on new responsibilities. One executive who made the great leap forward from secretary to professional recommends: "Ask for every bit of work you can get, whether you think you can do it or not, because the chances are you can. If you're a good secretary, there are an awful lot of things you can do that nobody gives you a chance to. Don't be afraid to take a risk." Having all these new responsibilities under your belt will be a plus when it comes time to apply for a professional position. Amassing different skills from varied assignments indicates you've clearly outgrown the secretarial mold, and are seriously committed to becoming a professional.

As soon as you feel capable and qualified, apply for other jobs within the company. Often when you're already inside and know the organization, you may be preferred over someone from the outside. But if you find that you are being turned down, it may be a sign that the secretarial stereotype is working against you. In that case, try to get yourself "promoted" to a nonsecretarial title. Discuss the matter with your boss. And be prepared, perhaps, for a decrease in pay (secretaries are frequently paid higher salaries than people in beginning professional slots). But if getting a title like "Associate Production Manager" or "Junior Marketing Director" can insure you a direct line out of secretarydom, it may be worth taking that temporary dock in pay.

Moving out from a secretarial position is no easy task. In fact, it may be the toughest hurdle you'll have to clear in your career path. But by doing it, you'll gain the self-confidence and determination necessary for success.

Stand Up and Be Counted

Ask the most liberated feminist you know whether she believes in Prince Charming, and after launching into a fiery tirade against the notion, a slight smile may cross her lips, a blush may rise to her cheeks, and she may quietly admit that she'd leave hay for his horse outside her door any time.

Prince Charming, it seems, is still alive in the hearts of women. Even at the workplace, women sometimes long for the Prince to appear. Only this time in their fantasies, when he arrives at the corporate doorstep it's to satisfy their corporate, not romantic, interests. How else can we explain why a multitude of working women possess a "sit back and wait" attitude when it comes to promotions and raises?

Well, if you recognize yourself as one of those waiters, take heart. There is hope for you. Just put all thoughts of the Prince aside, and start taking your career future into your own hands.

Quite simply, the key to getting ahead is getting yourself noticed. That is, noticed as a person with aspirations toward a bigger and better position. Whom should you be actively impressing with this fact? The people in your corporation who wield the most power are the ones you want to reach. If you've chosen your mentor carefully, he or she might be one of those people, or at least might travel in the same circles with them and can draw you to their attention. If you don't have a mentor as yet, ask members of your network to point out the king or queen pins in your company's power structure.

Then start being visible.

Make sure you attend meetings where you know the higher-ups will be present. If you're not invited to one of those meetings, ask your boss if you can sit in on it (tell your boss that the meeting could provide a learning experience for you). If you are a bona fide participant, contribute to the discussion. Make sure you say something of substance; even an intelligent question will do. But don't run off at the mouth for the sake of being heard.

Take on projects the results of which will be viewed by those higher up. Usually those projects are ones dealing with money (such as an increase in profits or sales). But if you've just improved your office's efficiency, the results of which can't yet be measured in dollars and cents, inform those higher up of your accomplishment. In a memo, stake a prediction as to how much time and money your work will eventually save (next to profits, upper management loves hearing about savings).

Also, get involved in projects that cross department lines. Volunteering to be on the company holiday party committee (the project no one else would touch with a ten-foot pole) can probably put you in good stead with the people you want to impress.

Another way to become visible is to make a name for yourself in the field. You can do this easily by joining a professional association and becoming actively involved. Sign up to head a committee or give a speech. By doing these things you'll get publicity in the association's journals, trade publications, and your own company newsletter. Always make contact with these news outlets anytime you have something to blow your horn about.

Build yourself a reputation as a real go-getter within your own company. Let your boss know you can handle responsibility by taking on added tasks (the best place to look for more work is on your boss's desk, so help your boss cut down on his or her work load). Solve crises yourself; don't pass the buck. Take care of your own neck of the woods: if you'll be away on vacation, see that all your assignments are brought up to date, try to anticipate any problems that may arise while you're away and remedy them beforehand. You may think that these actions can impress only your boss. But word spreads. Soon your boss's boss, that person's boss, and members of upper management will have heard that you're a person to be valued and rewarded.

About the best way to get noticed is to exercise a little political savvy. What do we mean by that? Here's a good definition we've heard: "Savvy is taking the information that we have in the back of our head and bringing it up to the front of our mind and processing it." Still confused? Think of savvy as the ability to take advantage of the obvious.

For instance, one woman we heard of was seeking to move up from a secretarial position. She always used to take work home nights, but when she was at the office late one evening, she noticed a top executive toiling away. She then decided it was best for her to burn the evening oil in the office. After the fourth or fifth night she was there, this executive introduced himself. He asked her what she was working on. She told him about her project, and how grateful she was that it enabled her to learn about the various areas of the company. She told him of her desire to land a managerial position. Within a few weeks he brought her name to the attention of another corporate head, and she was made an internal consultant.

Last but not least, learn from experience—the experience of others. Ask the people in your company you admire and who've "made it" how they did it. Barbara Holt advises, "Look at people that have done it, and don't be afraid to ask them how. Learn from their strong points and also from their mistakes." One woman on her first job found herself without a mentor or a network. She realized the only strategy for herself was to find role models: "I just tried to copy the qualities of the people I admire, sort of twist them to fit my own personality." What she's come up with is her own style: a composite of the best she's seen in others and the best she's found in herself.

Even though all the signs are there that you want to be

promoted, unless you let others know what you want, you may not get it. The secretary who worked nights realized this; she told the executive just what she was after as soon as she got his ear. Again, don't just assume that your message is getting across. Get it across. Says Susan Moskowitz, a training specialist, "I'd have to say that the people who speak up move. Not that the ones who don't don't, but you pretty much make your own career."

And don't speak up just when an opening occurs. At that point it may be too late; your boss and the management might have someone else already pegged for the position. Let your boss know you want to get ahead in the company as soon as you're sure that that's what you want—for very often jobs are created for people. If management notices you have a special knack for dealing with people, for obtaining information from coworkers and getting them to finish assignments on time, they may create the position of "department manager" for you.

"You've got to be aggressive," says Portia Manley, a marketing analyst who works in the forest products industry. "Let a person know where you stand. I can remember one of my former bosses asking me, 'What would you have done if you couldn't have gotten in to interview with me for this job?' I said, 'I would've kept pounding on your door till I got in!' He said, 'Good, because a lot of my employees, if they can't do something the first time, will just sit back and end up staying in the same place for ten years instead of coming and pushing their way in to see me.' He told me that if you want to move ahead, you should let your supervisor know. Don't wait for your supervisor to tell you, 'Hey, I think it's about time for you to move on.' I think that's good advice."

So if you want to get ahead, the trick is to be *seen and heard*.

A Word of Caution on Promotions, or All That Glitters Is Not Gold

Although we've just told you that a promotion can pretty much be yours, let's for a moment get your feet firmly planted back on the ground. Hold off on ascending that ladder to success until you read the following.

A promotion is more than a spanking new title, your very first office, and a sizable increase in pay. A promotion usually entails a lot of hard work, added responsibilities, and more on-the-job stress. As one woman manager cannily observes, "There are not too many people who sit around and collect big, fat paychecks and do very little." Just as you worked extra hard to get promoted, you'll have to work even harder to keep your new position. Or as your grandmother put it, "You get nothing for nothing." She was right.

In a higher position you won't have the advantages you had on your first job. Mistakes you'll make will be highly visible and won't be excused because "you're still learning." You're supposed to have learned by the time you're promoted, and if you haven't, you at least have to hide the fact. And your boss won't be there to cover for you as much, or won't want to. So you pretty much have to fend for yourself. That pressure, along with your increased work load, can contribute to a lot of stress. If you're already coming home from work often feeling like a zombie, better find a way to cope. There'll be a lot of those zombielike days ahead.

A promotion can also eat into your free time, requiring you to work late hours, also weekends. How do you feel about losing part, if not all, of your social life? Would you mind traveling? As you go along in your career, always ask yourself how much getting ahead means to you, how much you're willing to give up for it, and where's the point you're going to say stop.

It's not that we're against promotions or corporate success. They're wonderful things, and provide a sense of personal fulfillment for many people. But since opportunities for success were denied women for so long, there's a lot of pressure for women to take on more and more. Personal *and* social pressure says you must succeed, you must get promoted, you must get ahead. And nobody has truthfully told women what's in store for them if they move up, what they stand to lose as well as gain. If you're out to get ahead, by all means forge onward. But always climb that ladder with open eyes, knowing full well what the next step will be like before your foot reaches it. And make sure you're ready. Take one step at a time, and you will be.

KNOW YOUR RIGHTS

You can't exercise your civil rights unless you know them. Here are two excellent booklets that will give you an overview of your rights as a working woman and tell you how you can get the government to enforce your civil rights—including employment, education, and credit rights. They are worth writing for; single copies are free.

A Working Woman's Guide to Her Job Rights from:

U.S. Department of Labor
Office of the Secretary
Women's Bureau
Washington, D.C. 20210

and

Getting Uncle Sam to Enforce Your Civil Rights
(Clearinghouse Publication #59) from:

Publications Division
U.S. Commission on Civil Rights
Washington, D.C. 20425

11

ON THE ROAD:
BUSINESS TRAVEL

YOUR BOSS HAS JUST asked you to fly out to Chicago to attend a meeting she won't be able to make. Your first reaction is fear ("What am I going to say to those people there?" and "I've never stayed alone in a hotel room before"). But those initial qualms will quickly give way to an emotional high that will stay with you until your return flight touches down on the runway.

Your first business trip is an important rite of passage that can give you a sense of having "arrived" in the business world. By sending you on a trip, your boss is letting you know you're now capable of representing the company to outsiders—potential clients, associates in the field, or the public at large. A successful first business trip can give you that sense of professionalism every person on her first job eagerly awaits. And it can lead to other on-the-job travel opportunities.

Newcomers to the travel scene can generally use a few pointers. And although we believe in learning from experience, when it comes to traveling it's best that you make as few "educational mistakes" as possible. Traveling is too important to your professional success to risk making too many blunders. So take the following advice on business travel to heart and you'll act—and feel—like a seasoned pro when you're on the road.

Planning Ahead

The first step to getting a smooth business trip off to a good start is to learn about the city (or cities) you will be visiting before you go. Talk to coworkers who have traveled there, read travel guides (for instance, *Get'em & Go Guide to America),* scan maps (some of the best are in the Rand McNally Road Atlas), and track down a copy of one of the local newspapers. Familiarizing yourself with a new city will be a great help when you sit down to make airline, hotel, and transportation arrangements with your company's in-house travel consultant or a travel agent. For instance, if you know beforehand that most of your business appointments are located in the central business district of the city, you can ask your travel adviser to make reservations for you in a hotel located in that immediate area. If you'll be visiting some suburban locales, you may need information about car rentals. When you're booking a flight or making train or bus reservations, give yourself adequate time. For instance, if your first meeting is in the morning, arrange to arrive the evening before so that you can get a good night's rest.

After you've made arrangements with your travel agent, the next step is to draw up an itinerary. This should include your travel schedule, arrival and departure dates, name(s) and telephone number(s) of your hotel(s), and a list of your appointments, including meetings, luncheons, or dinners. Be sure to jot down the time of each appointment, the complete address of the building or restaurant, and the names and telephone numbers of people you are meeting. Writing down your appointments can help you spot any potential problems and give you time to make any changes before you leave. It's a good idea to have another "eye" look at your schedule also. Madeline, a buyer for a New York department store, avoided some major gaffes by going over her itinerary for her first trip with her supervisor. "When I drew up my itinerary, I had simply assumed that Houston was geographically like New York, with a centrally located business district. I never checked a map either. I just went right ahead and lined up appointments back to back, figuring I could get from one to another in ten minutes' time. After reading my itinerary, my boss said the only way I'd ever make some of the appointments would be red-faced and forty minutes late, because they were located clear across town! I then made some quick phone calls and changed several meeting times."

If you're in need of more information (such as a company's floor number in an office building), don't be reluctant to call the people you will be meeting. Remember to take a copy of your itinerary with you and to leave one at your office and with anyone else who might need to reach you.

Cash and Carry

How much money should you take? Make a mental check of your trip, anticipating all the expenses that won't be charged directly to your company (like the hotel bill), or put on your credit card (a dinner for clients). Your in-transit expenses alone might include taxi fare to the airport, movie earphones on the plane, and a tip for the bellboy at the hotel. Daily food expenses will vary from city to city but you can estimate $4–$6 for breakfast, $6–$10 for lunch, and $15–$20 for dinner. Add up all your estimated expenses. Most companies will provide you with a cash advance to cover your travel expenses. But whether you use your company's advance or your own money (and get reimbursed later), take along at least $50 more than you think you'll need just in case you have any unforeseen expenses. It's a good idea to get all but $100 of your total estimated expenses in traveler's checks (denominations of $20 and $50 are best) that can be replaced if they are lost or stolen. It's also convenient to have at least $10 in one-dollar bills for tips, and about $5 in change in case you have to make any long-distance calls from a pay phone. (Keep tip and phone money in an outside pocket or change purse so that you won't have to rummage for it when you're in a hurry.)

Don't forget to take along "plastic money"—your credit cards. At least one nationally accepted bank card (like Visa or Mastercard) will enable you to pay for food and entertainment bills, rent a car, and will serve as identification if you wish to pay a bill by personal check. At the trip's end, your credit card statement will provide you with a clear, complete record of your expenses. If traveling is going to become a major part of your job, it may be worthwhile to apply for a travel and entertainment credit card also. (For more information about credit cards see page 221.)

Tracking Down Expenses

We're all familiar with the stereotype of a successful business person—someone with an unlimited travel expense account that enables him or her to stay at first-rate hotels and eat at *haute cuisine* restaurants every night. In reality, very few business people are allowed to live this regally when traveling. And they do have to account for whatever they spend. So resolve now to keep track of every nickel and dime you spend.

Before you leave, make sure you know what your company considers to be legitimate travel expenses. For instance, will you be allowed to take any business associates out to a night club? If you decide to travel with your own

car, will you get reimbursed for gas and toll charge
companies spell out their rules regarding travel expe
their company manual (including instructions on ho
complete an expense account and apply for cash advanc
If your company doesn't have a manual, ask your boss or
colleagues for the information.

To prepare yourself for the accounting paperwork awaiting you back at the office, keep track of what you spend
when you spend it. Molly, an aeronautics salesperson,
learned this the hard way. "On my first job I attended a
convention out west. It never occurred to me to keep a
running tally of my expenses. I figured I'd remember them
all when I got back to the office. But when I returned, I
stared at my expense report sheet and my mind went
blank—like the page in front of me." You can avoid this
problem by taking along a small notebook and writing down
all your expenses at the end of each day. Also stick an
envelope into the notebook to hold all your receipts. Find
out beforehand if you need to collect receipts on everything. Some companies, for instance, have a policy of
requesting receipts for bar, food, and entertainment expenses that are over $25. Other companies require a receipt
even for the charges made directly to them, such as airplane
tickets and hotels.

All the Clothing That's Fit to Pack

Whether you're going on a two-day business trip or a
seven-day, three-city whirl, you'll want to travel light. That
means taking along only the essentials. Separates—skirts,
blouses, and blazers—travel well, and give you the neat,
professional look you need. Choosing separates in one color
scheme will give you an opportunity to mix and match. Try,
if you can, to take seasonless fabrics—lightweight wools,
gabardines, and silk—which will prepare you for different

climates and will keep your bag light. (Also keep in mind that clothes with some synthetic fiber content are more wrinkle-resistant.) Find out in advance if any very "dressy" occasion is planned. (If you're not sure, throw in a suitable dress just in case.) Don't take along any new shoes; traveling is not the time to break them in. See that the shoes you do take (two pairs are all that will be needed) are the kind that can take you from day to evening—for instance, open-toed sandals or sling-backed pumps. How do you dress for a climate colder or warmer than that of your own city? Take along clothing that can be "added" or "subtracted" according to the temperature—sweaters, vests, blazers, and a lightweight raincoat. What should you wear on the plane or train? Opt for a business look, such as a suit. You'll get your trip off to a professional start by looking the part, and you'll have one less outfit to pack!

Aside from clothing, there are some other travel essentials. The following items are good investments, especially if there is more business travel in your future: an alarm clock, sewing kit, folding umbrella, blow dryer, collapsible skirt hangers, flashlight, and travel iron/steamer.

Don't forget to pack business essentials too. Take along a generous supply of business cards, note pads, envelopes, stamps, pens, pencils, paper clips, and tape. Check to see that you have all necessary correspondence and reports with you. Plan to ship any material in bulk ahead of time (for instance, copies of your company's annual report to distribute at a convention). If you are shipping material (charts, for example) for a presentation or speech, be sure you take along a copy or backup information with you in case the materials don't arrive on time. Ship home any printed matter you accumulate on your trip rather than having it weigh you and your luggage down.

As for luggage, pieces you can carry onto planes and trains are best. With carry-on luggage, you can avoid long waits at the baggage claim and also the worry about losing your belongings in transit. One compact suitcase (soft-sided luggage is very lightweight) and a small tote or garment bag should be all you need. (Many airlines now require that all carry-on luggage fit under the seats, so be sure your suitcase is small enough.)

Packing It In

Face it: wrinkled clothing will be a fate to contend with when traveling on business. Though you may have heard about packing tips guaranteed to make your outfits look dry-cleaner-fresh when you open your bags, in all likelihood your clothes won't arrive as neat and pressed as when you packed them. That's why you should take along a travel iron or steamer too. You can also plan on having your hotel send clothes out to the dry cleaner as soon as you arrive. In an emergency, hanging up clothing in a steam-filled bathroom can help beat the wrinkles.

There are a few travel tips that do help you avoid many of the wrinkles. Pack all your bulky items like shoes and hair dryers first. Place them along the hinge sides of your bag so they'll be nearest to the ground when you carry the bag and won't crush your lightweight items. Roll up all your no-wrinkle clothes, like underwear, nightgowns, and sweaters to form a cushioning bottom layer. On top, place everything that requires careful folding—like your skirts and blouses. Make as few folds as possible. You can also put plastic or tissue paper between these layers to protect against wrinkles. (Old dry cleaning bags work well.) Fill in all the extra spaces in your suitcase with belts, hosiery, and small items like your alarm clock or night light. Don't close your suitcase until the last minute; there's always something you remember to take with you five minutes before you head out the door!

Check-in Time

When you arrive at your hotel, you should expect two things: a reservation and a room that meets with your satisfaction. If you have written confirmation of your reservation, you can pretty well count on a room being available. But sometimes hotels do overbook and you can find yourself without a room. If this happens, it is up to the hotel to find you comparable accommodations at another hotel, pay for your cab fare there (and back again once a room does open up) and any phone calls you have to make as a result of this inconvenience. If the hotel staff doesn't make an effort to locate a room elsewhere, you can get in touch with your company travel adviser, who will have more clout in dealing with the hotel management. (Your company, for instance, can threaten to withdraw all future business from that hotel.)

Make sure your hotel room meets your standards. Look around the room carefully. Check that it's clean (especially peek into the bathroom), that the television, air conditioner, and curtain pulls work, and that a double lock and chain are on the door. Ask the bellboy to wait while you make your inspection. If you are pleased with what you see, send him off with a dollar tip. If you're unsatisfied with the room, call the assistant manager. He or she is the hotel trouble-shooter, the one to see if you have any complaints. The assistant manager will probably suggest another room; if not, convey your dissatisfaction with the present room and suggest they find you another. (Again, get in touch with your home office if the hotel management remains uncooperative.)

Once you have a chance to settle into your room, find out what services the hotel offers. Stop by the information desk and obtain a brochure that tells you where everything—from the beauty salon to the swimming pool—is located. Contact the hotel switchboard to ask if there are any messages for you. Make sure the operator has the correct room number and spelling of your name. Alert the switchboard to certain calls you will be expecting and where to locate you if you plan to be out.

Finally, take time to unwind totally. According to Marcia Vickery Wallace, travel editor at *Bride's* magazine, "It's especially important to pamper yourself while traveling—so indulge in whatever it is that makes you feel good." That may mean a shower and a nap, or maybe five minutes of sheer relaxation in the hotel sauna. You should get a fresh start before tackling any business appointments.

Tipping

It seems that most businesswomen are tip-happy. They've even gained a reputation of being the second biggest category of tippers (couples are the first). Why? Well, it isn't because they're making more money than men and therefore can afford to give it away. Rather, many believe that tipping generously is the only way women can be assured of receiving quality treatment on the road. "I've been traveling for fifteen years," says Wilma, an engineering consultant, "and fifteen years ago, there were few women on the road. I was put in some pretty shoddy rooms, and had to eat next to a lot of restaurant kitchens. I learned pretty quickly that tipping could make a difference. Now with a lot more women traveling, we're getting better treatment. But I still can't break my old habit of tipping heavily."

Since you don't have any old habits to break, start off on the right foot where tipping is concerned. "Don't feel you have to tip any more than a man would," advises Marcia Wallace. "Always tip according to effort; just don't throw a lot of money around." Suppose you ask your hotel doorman to get you a cab. If there's a whole line of cabs waiting outside the hotel, his effort consists only of motioning to the next driver in line and for this service you really don't have to tip at all. But if he went into the street and actually flagged down a cab for you, a fifty-cent tip would be in order. As for maid service, leave a dollar each day in a place where your maid will find it (for instance, on a pillow), instead of waiting to leave a cumulative tip at the end of your stay. Maids may change overnight in a big city hotel, and by leaving a daily tip you know it will go to the maid who actually cleaned your room that day.

Eating Right

One of your biggest fears about business travel may be how you're going to face eating alone. Some of the most assertive, independent businesswomen dread the thought of eating alone, and order from room service every night while they're traveling. While there's nothing wrong with eating in your room, you should make an effort to treat yourself to a restaurant every now and then.

How do you choose a restaurant? Hotel restaurants are generally the most accessible but check the local restaurants as well. Ask the business people you're visiting for recommendations. Take the opportunity to try a regional restaurant. Sample Cajun cuisine in New Orleans or Mexican food in California. Most travel experts suggest that you also check the lighting. Restaurants with medium lighting are best for a woman alone. Restaurants that are garishly lit or those that are dark and romantic can be depressing atmospheres for a woman on her own. Whatever your choice, call ahead for a reservation.

When you arrive at the restaurant, don't feel as if you must tip the maître d' extravagantly in order to get a good table and good service. Wait to tip him or her on your way out. (Two or three dollars is suggested.) If you are shown a table that is not to your liking, speak up. Say to the maître d', "This seems a little too dark [or noisy or small]. Could I sit over there?" Having your business card in hand at the time can add a little more punch to your request. Once you're seated, show interest in the menu and the wine list; ask the maître d' and waiter questions. "A restaurant staff likes to know their patrons care about food," says travel editor Marcia Wallace. "If you act interested, you're bound to get good service and attention."

If you're worried that you'll be left twiddling your thumbs between courses (and looking very lonely), take a book or magazine with you. However, service for one is generally speedier than you'd think. Don't plan on racing through your meal; eat slowly and take the time to clear your head and relax—something you couldn't do if you had to engage in small talk with company. Look around at the other diners. You'll probably see businesswomen like yourself eating alone, and enjoying their food and solitude. Your whole attitude about eating alone can definitely change for the better.

Remember, too, you probably won't be eating alone every night. You're sure to be joined by your business hosts on one or two evenings. And you may want to return the invitation. The ticklish part about taking your hosts out to dinner is that although they'll be flattered by your gesture, they're likely to reach for the check nonetheless. To avoid any awkwardness, plan ahead. Tell the maître d' to instruct the waiter to give you the check when the meal is over. If you're eating in your hotel's dining room, the maître d' can charge the meal directly to your room bill, and the check will never reach your table. Just in case any of your guests is so gauche as to ask, "Whatever happened to the check?" simply smile and say, "It's been taken care of."

Evenings Out

You may find that dining out will be the only evening activity you'll have time or energy for on your business trip. But if you're the type who can't go a few days without some entertainment, you'll want to seek out a play, movie, or concert during your evening hours. If you go out alone during the evening, play it safe and take a taxi to and from your destination—even if your hotel is in an area where you'd feel comfortable walking around.

Safety should be a paramount concern to you while you're traveling. Don't be paranoid, just be aware. When you come in at night, try not to enter a hotel elevator alone. Have your room key ready in your hand so you don't have to search for it in front of the door. Once you are in your room, lock and chain your door and never open it without knowing for sure who's there. Exercising a few precautions can go a long way toward protecting you when you're traveling alone.

Of Men and Myths

You may have heard all those stories about men you'll encounter while traveling. During the day they're as gallant as Sir Galahad, but in the evening they turn into wolves on the prowl. Well, we've heard verifications of this story. But we've also heard enough to confirm our belief that more on-the-road hanky-panky occurs in people's minds than in boardroom or bedroom suites. Such tales of travel hijinks reflect badly on both men and women.

You will be spending a lot of time with men—office colleagues accompanying you on your trip, or clients and associates you're visiting. Your days will find you working, lunching, and going out together. And it's very natural that this constant companionship will foster a certain degree of intimacy. Certainly no one expects you to talk shop all day; you and your colleagues would be terribly bored if you did. You can expect to enjoy yourself and have a good time with your business colleagues. But there should be enough room in any professional relationship for friendly feelings to develop without its necessarily turning into a romantic relationship.

What happens if a friendly relationship goes a step further and you do get a "loaded invitation"? Well, behave as you would back home. If you don't want the relationship to go beyond the platonic, say so. It can be awkward to turn someone down—especially a business colleague. You may want to avoid reaching the point where someone makes a pass at you by following a good rule: always end your evening in a public place, never in your room or your colleague's. Let's say you have dinner with a client in your hotel restaurant. At meal's end, he offers to escort you back to your room. You can politely reply, "Thanks, but it won't be necessary. I had a very enjoyable evening," and say good night in the hotel lobby.

What about asking a man to your room for a drink, a seemingly innocent and aboveboard gesture? While it may be simply a friendly gesture on your part, it can also be taken as a sign that more than a drink will be offered. And once the signals get confused, it can turn into an awkward and embarrassing situation for both of you. Valerie, a systems analyst for a Minnesota company, had one such embarrassing episode during her first business trip. "It was late at night and I was watching TV when Mark, a colleague traveling with me, knocked on my door. I let him in because I thought he came to discuss the project we were working on. As it turned out, he had a bottle of gin and two glasses in his hands. I sat on the bed and he sat on a chair. I started staring at the TV very intently in an attempt to ignore him. All the while my mind was racing, 'How am I going to get him out of here, what will I say to him?' Next thing I knew he had moved over to my bed and was pulling all these moves. I just turned around and said, 'Look, we're out on business, and I don't mix business with pleasure.' I felt like such an idiot saying that, but it was the only thing I could think of. It did work—he left.''

If you get into a situation like Valerie's in which someone makes a pass at you, the important thing is to be polite but firm. "Try to act grown-up about it the next morning; don't hold it against him," suggests Marcia Wallace. "After all, you'll be dealing with the person for the rest of the trip." If you give him a cold shoulder or act visibly angry, other people in your traveling circle may wonder what's wrong.

As for any temptations you may have to take a man up on his offer—that's a choice only you can make. But it's important that you consider the range of potential consequences of any decision you make. Most businesswomen advise against romantic involvements during business trips. Why? An affair could prove damaging to you professionally. Though you may think that no one will ever learn about your behavior miles away from the office, it's not always so. Word about "indiscretions"—particularly a woman's—often leaks out. (The old double standard is still alive and well.) What's more, the man who may be "safe" to get involved with today could one day end up as your boss or subordinate. It can put a strain on any professional relationship. And getting involved with the "wrong" person could put a company off limits to you in the future. So think carefully before you agree to any on-the-road involvement.

Homeward Bound

To get the last leg of your business trip off without a hitch, here are some things to keep in mind. Always give the airport a call to reconfirm your reservations. If your return flight was left open, it is especially important to get in touch with the airport early in your stay to make a reservation. Be sure you know what time you must check out of your hotel room. If your plane or train leaves early in the morning, plan on settling your hotel account the night before.

Stop by your hotel's information desk to ask if an airport limousine service is available, and the times it makes passenger pick-ups. Otherwise call a taxi service to arrange for a cab. Before leaving your room, check all closets, drawers, and furniture tops to make sure you haven't left anything behind. If you deposited any valuables in the hotel's safe deposit boxes, be sure to reclaim them before leaving.

When you arrive back at the office, send thank-you notes to the people you visited. Tell them what a pleasure it was to meet and work with them, and thank them for showing you any city sights or taking you to dinner. It's a gesture that can make a lasting impression on people and help keep your business relationship with them on good terms.

You'll probably be expected to draw up a memo or report to let your boss or colleagues know what you accomplished on your trip. Once you've done that, and finished filling out your expense account, take the time to write a memo to yourself about your first business trip. Think about what you learned about traveling. Remember all the things you did right (like arriving on time for all your appointments), and what you should have done better (like making more time in your schedule to relax). Make a note of the clothing that really worked for you—what you could have left behind and what you could have used. Place this memo in a folder and file it away. Read it before your next business trip. And when you return from that trip, be sure to amend it. Happy travels!

YOUR MONEY

12

"I don't care too much for money, for money can't buy me love. . . ."

THE BEATLES

THE BEATLES WERE RIGHT. Money can't buy you love. It also can't buy you happiness, world peace, inner peace, friendship, safety, health, or wisdom. However, money *can* buy certain necessities—"little things" like food, clothing, and shelter.

It used to be considered "unfeminine" to talk, think, or worry about money; ladies simply didn't soil their hands with the stuff. Thanks to this kind of Neanderthal thinking, many women still have "money anxiety" today. They cringe at the thought of asking for a raise and think of financial planning as something to be done "in the future."

Well, the future is here. There's nothing ladylike about being poor, cold, or hungry. And unless you're (a) an heiress, (b) a "kept" woman (shame on you!), or (c) living on a South Sea island with food from the trees and no utilities to pay, money is something you *must* be concerned about. And it's a concern that should not make you feel guilty. As Ruth Halcomb points out in her book, *Women Making It:*

Women can derive real satisfaction from achieving economic goals that they've set for themselves. Having economic goals doesn't mean we must become mindless worshippers of the "bitch goddess," as males metaphorically call money. But living in our present society we need money goals along with career planning to have the kind of life we want. Money goals, like career goals, must derive from our own values and reflect our real needs.

Maybe back in the Dark Ages we could count on learning the value of a dollar at our parents' knees. But general economic conditions and inflation have assured that everyone, including parents, Presidents, and Congress, is confused about what a dollar *is* worth. "One reason that a lot of young people get into debt early," according to Gerard Lareau, president of Consumer Credit Counseling Service, "is that parents simply don't talk about money. More young people are naive about personal finance than ever before. When they get their first paychecks, they are misled—it looks grand. Suddenly they have to pay for rent, mortgage, food, etc. . . . , and the paycheck's gone."

It's up to you to educate yourself about the ins and outs of personal money management in order to get the most value out of the dollars you do earn. It will also be your responsibility to learn as much as you can about your legal rights. In the past many women, both single and married, found it very difficult to obtain credit. There are new laws now that can help you, but only if you know your rights and exercise them.

Budgeting

General Motors does it. Catalyst does it. Your mother probably did it. "Budgeting is absolutely essential," says Mary Quinn of the National Foundation for Consumer

Credit. "Just as one has health care, one should have financial care as well."

A budget is simply a blueprint for how you will spend, or save, the money you earn. It can be as detailed or as sketchy as you want. But the more carefully planned your budget, the more control you will have over your finances and your life. Budgets are very personal; don't draw up your budget according to what your friend Mary Jane spends each month. A budget won't work unless it's tailored to you—to your life-style, needs, and wants.

When you draw up your budget, it helps to keep your goals in mind, whether they are short-term ones like saving up to go skiing for the weekend or long-term ones such as buying a home. Goals can help you stick to a budget because they will be your "reward" for being conscientious about your finances.

One budgeting hint that's especially helpful for first-jobbers is to open a checking account. Keeping a checkbook can help you (1) by keeping cash out of your pocket (thus making you think before you spend it) and (2) by serving as a record of not only the amount going out but also where it's going.

How Much Do You Really Earn?

Ten, twelve, and fifteen thousand dollars a year are sums that promise a lot but deliver—what? What you earn and what you take home are two different things. Your *gross salary* may be $11,000 a year but your *net income* will be at least 15 to 20 percent less, due to a plethora of deductions tacked onto every American's paycheck. For instance: federal, state, and in some cases, city income tax; union dues; social security contributions (FICA); disability; group insurance; and any other deductions your particular employer makes—for instance, a payroll savings plan. Look at your weekly paycheck stub to find out how much is being deducted. Use your *net income* when you plan your budget, because that's the actual amount of cash you have to spend.

The basic tenet of budgeting is to make sure that the money you have coming in doesn't exceed the money going out. In other words, don't spend more than you earn. In drawing up your budget, the first step is to figure out how you're spending your money now. This means itemizing your expenses. A three-month period is the best indicator of where your money is going. Note: seasonal changes can drastically increase expenses (for example, for heat or air conditioning, vacations, Christmas gifts, etc.). If you have a hard time remembering what you've spent, look over your old checkbook stubs, canceled checks, receipts, or any old bills you may have kept. If you're fairly new at the money-management game and don't have very many records, resolve now to keep track of *all* your expenses for the next month or so. Buy yourself a small notebook and write down every purchase you make.

Expenses can be divided into two broad categories: *fixed expenses,* which are regular monthly expenses that you can anticipate, such as rent and utilities, and *flexible or day-to-day expenses,* those which vary from week to week or month to month. Food, for example, is a variable expense depending on how often you eat out, how much you entertain, or how many people you feed. Keep track of how much you spend on food in a week, and then multiply by four to get a monthly estimate.

Some fixed expenses don't occur monthly. For instance: real estate taxes, tuition, or car insurance payments. But you should set aside a certain amount of money *each month* so that when these bills *are* due, you know you have the money to pay them. (You can even put this money in a savings account, earning interest, until it's time to pay the bills.)

Savings should also be a part of your monthly budget. A nest egg can add much to your emotional and financial peace of mind—it's your emergency reserve. Most financial experts suggest that you keep at least three months' salary in your savings account. If you are positively allergic to the thought of savings, find out if your company has a payroll savings plan. Under these plans a certain amount is deducted from your paycheck and automatically deposited in a savings account. Some banks will also automatically transfer a fixed amount from your checking to your savings account each month if you request it.

Remember your goals. Suppose you've decided that you need $1000 to go on vacation next year. Well, put a certain amount of money into your budget each month so that you'll be sure to attain that goal.

Following are some of the basic expenses you might include in your budget:

Monthly Expenses

Rent or mortgage payments

Utilities
electricity
heating
water
telephone

Food

Clothing
(including laundry and dry cleaning)

Insurance
car
life
health/medical
home/property

Education
  tuition
  books and supplies
  educational loan payments

Transportation
  bus/train/subway fare
  gas/tolls/parking
  car maintenance

Debts
  credit charges
  other
  car payments

Medical/dental

Taxes (not withheld)

Personal
  toiletries
  haircuts
  entertainment
  magazines/books/newspapers
  other

Again, budgets are very personal. You may want to include other items in your monthly spending plan—for instance, contributions to religious and/or political organizations, gifts, travel, etc. You're the only one that can know how you want to spend your money.

When you've listed all your expenses, subtract this total from your *monthly net income.* Are you satisfied with your spending plan? Do you want to "redistribute" funds in any way? If your expenses exceed your income, you must reevaluate your spending patterns. Where can you cut down? Flexible expenses are easiest to trim. For instance, it's much cheaper to bring your lunch from home than it is to eat out every day. Reading magazines and books in the library is less expensive than buying them all. Taking advantage of sales and using weekly newspaper coupons at the supermarket can also be dollar-savers.

If you have money left over at the end of the month, congratulations! This money is your "discretionary income," money you can spend on whatever you want. Maybe you want to add a little more to your clothing budget, or take in a few more movies each month. Or you could buy a savings bond, or invest the money some other way. Increasing your savings is very wise.

Keep working at your budget until you get the plan that's right for you. And remember to revise it periodically. If the rent goes up or you get a raise, be sure to include the change in a revised budget.

Taxes

Remember the old saying that the only two certainties are death and taxes? Well, putting aside death for the moment, April 15 does have a habit of coming around regularly every year. And sometimes it manages to creep up on us before we know it.

Income tax forms can be boring, confusing, and certainly a nuisance to fill out. But whether you do your own return, sign a joint return, or get someone else to do the dirty work, you owe it to yourself to learn a little about the 1040 and its friends—even if only to see how much money Uncle Sam is getting from you now.

If you've been lucky enough never to have filled out a tax return before, the worst thing you can do is wait until April 14 to find out how. It's a sure way of getting an ulcer before you're thirty. Sometime *before* "D-day" (preferably several months before), call your local IRS office for a copy of Publication #17, *Your Federal Income Tax.* It comes complete with a sample 1040 form.

It is possible to fill out your own tax form, especially if you have a fairly simple tax return without elaborate deductions. As a first-jobber, you're more than likely to fall into the "fairly simple" category. (We mean your tax return, of course.) And Uncle Sam and the IRS are always willing to lend a hand. The IRS (in keeping with the it's-better-to-give-than-to-receive spirit), offers free advice for "taxed" taxpayers. They maintain a toll-free telephone information line (look in the Yellow Pages), with representatives who can answer questions about taxes and forms. Or you can visit them in person. The IRS will not fill out the tax form for you, but they will answer specific questions and generally nudge you in the right direction. It's a good idea to look over Publication #17 and try your hand at filling out a sample form before you go; that way, you'll know what questions to ask.

If you wait until April 14 to get help from the IRS, be prepared for long lines and long waits. As April 15 closes in, the legions of last-minute taxpayers increase and multiply. Go early if you want more personal attention and time. If you're planning to itemize deductions on your tax form (instead of taking the standard deduction), be sure to take along copies of documents that substantiate your claims.

Many more deductions other than the standard business lunches we've all heard about are permitted. Here are some "deductibles" you may not be aware of:

- Interest charges on bank credit cards, revolving charge accounts, installment purchases.

- Dues to unions or professional organizations.

- Medical examinations required by your employer.

- Items prescribed by a doctor—drugs, eyeglasses, contact lenses, birth control pills.

- Special uniforms or equipment required by your employer that cannot be adapted to personal use (for instance, you can't wear a nurse's uniform or a fire officer's uniform to mow the lawn on Saturday).

- Trade and professional magazine subscriptions related to your work.

- Employment agency fees (even if they don't find you a job), if you're seeking employment in your *present* career field.

- Expenses for typing and printing a résumé and postage for mailing copies to possible employers—again, you must be seeking employment in your present field.

- If you use a portion of your home "exclusively" and "regularly" for business, you may be able to deduct a portion of the rent, utilities, repairs, and insurance you pay.

- Educational expenses (tuition, books, lab fees, etc.) that are related to your job or that improve or refresh job skills (you cannot deduct expenses if the education is to qualify you for a new career).

These deductions are just a few of those allowed. In most cases certain conditions must be met, and you must keep careful records to prove your claims. If you think you may be able to itemize your deductions and want more information, consult the following publications available free from the IRS:

#529—*Miscellaneous Deductions and Credits*
#508—*Educational Expenses*
#587—*Business Use of Your Home*
#502—*Medical and Dental Expenses*
#463—*Travel, Entertainment and Gift Expenses*

The IRS maintains that if you earn up to $20,000 and your income derives primarily from earnings, stocks, bonds, or interest, you can probably handle the 1040 by yourself. However, if your financial situation is more complex or you feel you want or need more help than the IRS can give you, professional tax services can conquer your tax forms—for a fee.

Certified Public Accountants (CPA's), lawyers, and "enrolled agents" (former IRS agents with five or more years' experience or individuals that have passed strict examinations given by the U.S. Treasury Department) can all represent you before the IRS and negotiate or make settlements on your behalf in case you have the good fortune of being audited. They cannot advertise their services. However, don't count on these practitioners to fill out your 1040; they are reluctant to do uncomplicated personal returns because it is a seasonal business and not very profitable for them.

You're probably familiar with the commercial tax preparers such as H & R Block, Beneficial Income Tax Service (a subsidiary of Beneficial Finance Company), and Tax Corporation of America. They all fill out individual tax returns, including the short 1040. Some small bookkeeping companies, private individuals, accountants, and noncertified public accountants also prepare returns. All can advertise their services. These preparers can accompany you to an IRS audit interview, but they can answer questions only about the actual work done on your return. They cannot negotiate settlements, argue points of law or tax regulations, or appeal your case before the IRS.

Fees will vary depending on the section of the country you live in, the preparer, the complexity of your return, or the time spent on it. You're advised to shop around and settle the fee for the service in advance. In this case, cheaper is not necessarily better, and quality will count.

If you're considering going to a commercial tax-preparation company, inquire about the training their preparers have and how long they've been in business, and try to talk to some of their previous clients. If you are going to pay an individual to do your return, it's particularly important that you talk with someone who knows the individual and can attest to his/her integrity and skill. No formal training or diploma is needed to become a tax preparer; so it's up to you to do some investigating and checking of qualifications and track records.

How Do You Get Credit?

Credit is a privilege granted by a bank, store, or other institution, enabling a consumer to borrow money or defer payment for goods, services, or property until a later date. We're all familiar with plastic credit cards, but credit also includes bank loans, cash advances, overdraft checking privileges, dealer installment plans, and mortgage loans. Other agencies that extend credit include savings and loan associations, credit unions, finance companies, life insurance companies, some employers, and oh yes, loan sharks.

Who needs credit? Everyone does. Used properly, credit can be a useful tool. Credit can help you finance your education, a new home, or a car. With credit you can make major purchases such as furniture, stereos, or televisions without having to carry a lot of money with you. Credit also enables you to buy and use an item before you have the cash in hand to pay for it. It enables you to borrow money in cases of financial emergency too. In addition, credit cards are useful ID's for cashing checks, and they enable you to make many purchases over the telephone.

If credit is so wonderful, why do so many consumers experience difficulty with it? People get into trouble when they start thinking of credit as an addition to their paychecks or as "extra" money. It's not. Whether you're using your charge card to pay for a new sweater, or applying to the bank for a car loan, credit is simply borrowed money—money you must pay back sooner or later. And the longer it takes to pay, the more it will cost you because interest and finance charges on unpaid bills can run up to quite a high sum.

Why should a bank lend you $1000? What makes a department store trust you with that little plastic card? An agency's decision to extend credit is based on their evaluation of your "credit-worthiness," your ability and willingness to repay a debt. What makes you credit-worthy? Creditors examine several characteristics in a potential borrower. They look for indications of "stability"—employment at one company for a certain length of time, ownership of a house or apartment, residence in one city or dwelling for some length of time, and existence of a phone in a borrower's home. Checking and savings accounts are also signs of stability, and so is "reliable" income—reliable in this case meaning continuous. (NOTE: Under the Equal Credit Opportunity Act [ECOA], reliable income can mean income derived primarily from stocks and bonds and income from part-time work, child support, alimony, pension annuities, retirement benefit programs, or public assistance. The creditor *may* ask you to prove that this income has been received consistently.) Creditors also take into account comments from any personal references, and any assets you own, for example, life insurance policy cash value, securities, real estate, and personal property.

Another very important consideration in granting credit is your credit history, the record of how you've handled your ongoing financial obligations, or, to put it simply, how you've paid your bills in the past. Credit histories are kept by over 2500 credit bureaus in the United States. Bureaus are sometimes owned jointly by merchants and lenders; they may be privately owned or owned by a few institutions that make services available to nonmembers in the community.

Some consumers make the mistake of thinking that credit bureaus rate people as good or bad credit risks. They do not. Credit bureaus simply collect information about you from other creditors with whom you've dealt previously and from public records. Notations made on your credit report include your line of credit on credit accounts (for instance, your $500 limit on VISA), record of payment or delinquency on previous loans, payment patterns on installment purchases, legal action to enforce collection of debts, any civil judgments, defaults, repossessions, and bankruptcy.

Starting Your Own Credit History

If you've always paid for everything in cash and have never taken out a loan, you probably don't have a credit history. How do you start one? Well, it takes time; you'll have to start in a small way and build up slowly. It's sometimes harder for recent college graduates to begin getting credit, since they usually haven't been working very long or may have recently moved into a new home. But some creditors will take a chance on younger people because they'd like to get them as regular customers.

Gerard Lareau of Consumer Credit Counseling Service and Mary Quinn, director of counseling services at the National Foundation for Consumer Credit, offer the following guidelines for starting your credit history:

- First, get a checking and small savings account in your own name. (If you're married and share a joint account, make certain the account is established in *both* names—Mary Doe and John Doe, not Mr. and Mrs. John Doe.) Savings and checking accounts are not part of your credit history, but they serve to establish your financial identity and are seen as a sign of stability by creditors.

- Apply for department store and gasoline credit cards. There are many different types of store accounts; the most common is the monthly account you must pay in full within thirty days. After that, you're charged an interest rate on the unpaid balance. (Or you can also arrange to make an installment purchase. You pick the length of payment period you want, usually 12, 18, or 36 months, and then sign an agreement with the store that you'll pay for the purchase in equal installments plus interest.)

- After you've used these cards for a while, apply for bank cards such as Mastercard and VISA, the two most common bank cards. Since each bank has its own guidelines for deciding credit-worthiness, it's possible to be refused a card by one bank and granted one by another. So keep trying. Mastercard and VISA are revolving charge accounts. You do not pay a finance charge if your bill is paid in full within the first 25 to 30 days of billing date. Thereafter the Annual Percentage Rate (APR) on your unpaid balance is 1½ percent per month, or up to 18 percent per year.

- When you are issued a card, the bank will indicate your line of credit, the maximum amount you are allowed to charge, based on your credit-worthiness. If you continue to prove credit-worthy (i.e., pay your bills regularly and on time), your line of credit can be extended at your request or sometimes automatically.

Retail and bank cards are not the only kinds of credit cards. There are also the travel and entertainment cards such as American Express, Diner's Club, Carte Blanche, and the airline industry cards. These cards are harder to get and usually have a certain minimum income requirement, generally around $12,000. You are charged an annual fee of $20 to $35 for these cards. There is no spending limit, and you are expected to pay your bill in full every month. (After that they add on a delinquency charge of about 1½ percent on your unpaid balance.) These cards also offer extra "goodies" such as travel insurance, overnight replacement of lost or stolen cards, travel magazines, and traveler's checks.

Using retail and bank cards is one of the easiest and cheapest ways to begin a credit history, because you can use them "free" if you pay your bills within the specified length of time. However, it takes time to build up credit this way. You can speed up establishing your credit-worthiness a little by asking for a small loan, but it will "cost" you extra— you'll have to pay interest. If you borrow against the security of your bank account, the interest you pay on the loan will be partly offset by the interest your account keeps on earning. Or you could ask for a loan and deposit it immediately into your savings account. That way, you'll still be earning interest on the deposit as you pay off the loan. Since the purpose of the loan will be to establish a good credit history, make sure you stick to your part of the bargain. "Always pay back debts on time," says Gerard Lareau of the CCCS. "That's what they really look at. 'Pay as agreed' is the slogan used in credit. And watch out for too many credit cards too soon. Having them in plain sight is a temptation." Creditors also become wary if you have too much access to credit.

If you have trouble getting credit at first, you could ask a relative or friend who has a good credit standing to cosign your loan or credit application. If you do get a cosigner, remember that he or she will be sharing your liability and will be legally responsible for paying your debt if you default. Don't apply for credit unless you can afford it.

If You're Denied Credit

You've been denied a credit card or the loan you applied for. Why? If you're young and on your first job, it could be for several reasons:

- You may not have been working at your job or living at your present address long enough.
- Your income may be too low to support the loan or credit requested.
- Your cosigner cannot afford extra liabilities.

If you have too much to pay on outstanding accounts or loans (for example, an educational loan), or if your credit history contains erroneous information (not an unusual occurrence), you may also be denied credit.

Under the law a creditor is obliged to notify you, within 30 days, of action taken on your credit application. If you are denied credit, a creditor must: (1) give you the specific reasons why credit was denied, or inform you of your right to request the specific reasons in writing; (2) include a statement of your rights under the Equal Credit Opportunity Act; and (3) inform you of the name and address of the federal agency that would handle any complaints that you might have.

If you are dissatisfied with a creditor's reasons for denial of credit and believe that you're credit-worthy, under the Fair Credit Reporting Act of 1973 you are entitled to see the credit bureau report used to evaluate your credit application. Ask the lender which credit bureau they use and write to them. If you want a free copy of your credit report, you must request it within thirty days of the initial rejection letter. After that you are still entitled to request the information, but you'll be charged a fee ranging from $3 to $5.

You can correct negative information that appears on your credit history (for example, if you're involved in a dispute with a creditor). When you get your credit report, you are entitled to enter an explanatory statement of one hundred words or less. Identify the creditor and the facts of the dispute. Your statement of explanation must accompany your records whenever information is requested on you for review in future credit applications.

If there is incorrect information in your credit file, you are legally entitled to ask the bureau to recheck any information that you question. If the information *is* incorrect, the bureau must immediately remove it from your file and notify all creditors who have received the erroneous information about the correction. (Be sure to make copies of any correspondence to your creditors or to the credit bureau.)

Whenever you make a correction on your report or enter an explanatory statement, you should wait a few weeks and then request another copy of your credit report. Make certain that the corrections have been made accurately and to your satisfaction.

If you've been denied credit because of inaccuracies in your credit report, you can reapply to creditors when the report has been corrected. Remember that different lenders have varying lending policies and guidelines of creditworthiness; so you can apply to several different creditors. If you're still denied credit and have followed all the proper procedures, you can get in touch with the local, state, or federal authority that governs the particular lender. If you're unsure of which agency it is, call your state division of human rights or any consumer protection agency listed under your state's Banking Division.

For More Information

The Federal Reserve Board in Washington, D.C. is a good source of consumer information. They distribute copies of the Equal Credit Opportunity Act (ECOA) and publish a series of very helpful consumer-education pamphlets, including *The ECOA and Women, How to File a Consumer Credit Complaint,* and *Consumer Handbook to Credit Protection Laws.* For a list of all their publications write:

Board of Governors of the Federal Reserve System
20th and C Streets, NW
Washington, D.C. 20551
Attn: Publications Department

The National Foundation for Consumer Credit distributes many consumer-information publications. They also publish a Directory of Consumer Credit Counseling Services in the United States and Canada. For more information write:

National Foundation for Consumer Credit
1819 H Street, NW
Suite 510
Washington, D.C. 20006

The Consumer Credit Project in Illinois publishes an excellent booklet called *New Credit Rights for Women* that covers everything you'd ever need to know about credit—

and more. It is available for $2.00 (plus $.75 postage and handling) from:

Consumer Credit Project
261 Kimberly
Barrington, Illinois 60010

The Consumer Credit Project also offers free counseling on credit discrimination and consumer protection laws, and they review complaints and refer consumers to the proper regulatory agencies.

Many local services throughout the country help consumers with financial planning. Local Y's, feminist credit unions, women's organizations, and community colleges offer courses, workshops, and counseling on many aspects of personal finances. You can also take a look at the many books currently published on personal finances and investments. (See the bibliography.) You owe it to yourself to be as well informed as possible; it's your money—and your life.

CREDIT QUIZ

How "credit-conscious" are you? Take the following quiz to find out. (Answers on page 232.)

TRUE OR FALSE

1. You must choose a courtesy title (Miss, Ms., Mrs.) on a credit form._____

2. A creditor may inquire about your birth control practices or plans to have children because these may affect your ability to repay a loan._____

3. Although you are credit-worthy, you may be denied credit because your husband is considered a bad credit risk._____

4. Income derived from part-time work is considered reliable income for the purposes of granting credit._____

5. Checking and savings accounts are not included in credit bureau reports._____

6. If your credit card is lost or stolen, your maximum liability for unauthorized use of the card is $50._____

7. The Truth in Lending Law prohibits credit card issuers from sending you a credit card unless you've requested or applied for it.__

8. A creditor may take as long as necessary to decide on your credit application.__

9. You can't review a credit bureau report unless you're filing a complaint against a creditor._____

10. A creditor may simply state, "You didn't meet our minimum requirements" as a valid reason for denial of credit._____

QUIZ ANSWERS

1. False.
2. False.
3. False, unless you are applying for a joint account.
4. True.
5. True.
6. True. In order to be liable for even that sum, the unauthorized use of your card must have occurred before you notified the card-issuer of loss or theft.
7. True.
8. False. A creditor must notify you within thirty days of any action taken on a credit application.
9. False. Anyone can review his/her credit report at any time.
10. False. The creditor must give you a specific reason, such as "Your income is insufficient," or "You haven't worked long enough," etc.

MARRIED WÓMEN'S CREDIT RIGHTS

Did you know that as recently as 1974, a married woman could not get credit in her own name? Creditors had a habit of assuming that women couldn't be counted on to continue working because they'd get pregnant, quit their jobs, and leave all their creditors high and dry. All reports to credit bureaus on accounts used by both husband and wife were made only in the husband's name. Women who divorced or became widowed were left with no credit history. "I can't tell you how many women were 'nonpersons.' They had no credit, or money. And the older you got, the harder it was," says Gerard Lareau of Consumer Credit Counseling Service.

As a result of the Equal Credit Opportunity Act, however, creditors now must report information on any account used by both husband and wife or on which both are liable *under each spouse's name.* Information on joint accounts must be kept in separate files, one for each spouse. (NOTE: Mrs. John Doe is *not* your legal name; it is merely a social title that a succession of women can claim. You have three choices: you can open or maintain your accounts in your first name and maiden name—Mary Smith; your first name and husband's surname—Mary Doe; or a combined surname—Mary Smith-Doe.)

If your marital status changes in any way, you can keep your own accounts and credit history. Unless there is a valid indication that you are no longer willing or able to pay your debt, a creditor may not

- ask you to reapply for credit
- close your account, or
- change the terms of your account.

A creditor may, however, ask you to reapply if you've relied on your husband's income to support your credit.

234 Making the Most of Your First Job

IF YOU CAN'T PAY THE BILL COLLECTOR

Suppose you've had some kind of financial emergency and can't make your credit payments. What can you do? First of all, *don't:* hide, exile yourself in Canada, or refuse to answer the phone or open your mail.

Do: protect yourself and your credit history. (It's best to have a copy of all correspondence with the creditor for your own records. This will protect you if the account changes hands, or if the person you were dealing with is no longer there. It will also help you if you're having trouble "fixing" your credit report later on.) Contact the credit manager, merchant, or lender. Explain fully the reason you can't meet your payments—whether it's illness, strike, loss of work, or some family emergency. Discuss the problem and your prospects for paying in the future with the creditor. A possible solution might be a temporary postponement of payment or a reduction in the size of payments. (Another possibility is a debt-consolidation loan. This type of loan lumps all your debts to different creditors into one lump sum. But the interest rates on this type of loan are generally very high.) You'll find that most creditors will be reasonable; they'd rather get their money late than have to take you to court to get it, or have you declare bankruptcy.

DANGER SIGNALS

Danger. It *can* happen to you. Once you're credit-worthy, you'll find that credit is much easier to get and use. And in these times of shrinking dollar values and rising inflation, it's very easy to fall into the buy-now-pay-later habit. What are some of the signals that tell you you're heading for trouble?

- You're spending 20 percent or more of your take-home pay on debt repayment.

- You're a month or more behind in your monthly installment payments.

- Your creditors are beginning to phone and write in order to collect their money.

- You're completely broke the week after receiving your paycheck.

- You've begun to pay only the minimum amounts on your credit card balances.

- You've completely emptied your savings account in order to make ends meet.

- You owe so many creditors that you've lost track of the total amount of money you owe.

- You've begun to charge groceries and other day-to-day expenses because you don't have the cash to pay for them.

CONSUMER CREDIT LAWS

To exercise your rights wisely, you must know them. Federal consumer credit laws offer you these major protections:

The Truth in Lending Act. Requires disclosure of the "finance charge" and the "annual percentage rate"—and certain other costs and terms of credit—so that you can compare the prices of credit from different sources. It also limits your liability on lost or stolen credit cards.

The Equal Credit Opportunity Act. Prohibits discrimination against an applicant for credit because of age, sex, marital status, race, color, religion, national origin, or receipt of public assistance. It also prohibits discrimination because you have made a good-faith exercise of any of your rights under the federal consumer credit laws. If you've been denied credit, the law requires that you be notified in writing and gives you the right to request the reason for the denial.

The Fair Credit Billing Act. Sets up a procedure for the prompt correction of errors on a credit account and prevents damage to your credit rating while you're settling a dispute.

The Fair Credit Reporting Act. Sets up a procedure for correcting mistakes on your credit record and requires that the record be kept confidential.

The Consumer Leasing Act. Requires disclosure of information that helps you compare the cost and terms of one lease with another and with the cost and terms of buying on credit or with cash.

The Real Estate Settlement Procedures Act. Requires that you be given information about the services and costs involved at "settlement," when real property transfers from seller to buyer.

The Home Mortgage Disclosure Act. Requires most lending institutions in metropolitan areas to let the public know where they make their mortgage and home improvement loans.

Pamphlets describing some of these laws in more detail are available from the Board of Governors of the Federal Reserve, or from the Federal Reserve Bank in your district.

(Reprinted from the Federal Trade Commission pamphlet *How to File a Consumer Credit Complaint.*)

Part IV

Looking Back, Looking Ahead

13

MOVING UP

REMEMBER HOW UTTERLY INCOMPETENT you were feeling when you had just started your job? You swore you'd be fired within your first six months as soon as your boss caught onto you. Well, those six months came and went, and somewhere along the line you not only became able to perform your work adequately, you even developed a certain expertise. That expertise hasn't lost its edge yet, but today the challenge of your work may have disappeared.

Although we all say we dread falling into a rut, a job that has become routine can be especially alluring sometimes. Here's why: once a job becomes mechanical, you're free to devote your energies to other areas of your life—family, romantic interests, leisure activities. Careers have a tendency to be all-consuming; the first job, with its countless pressures, is no exception. You've probably been looking forward to the time when you can go to work with your mind in "neutral." And now that it's come, you don't know how to handle it.

How Far Can You Go?

You never thought you'd hear yourself say it, but your work has become too easy for you. And you are beginning to worry. Worry you should. There comes a time in practically every job when life gets a bit too comfortable for your own good. For most people the first job begins to ease up by the second year. When you reach that point and your job does in fact become as easy as pie, indulge yourself and take advantage of this rest period. You deserve it. But don't let it go on for too long; grab onto that ladder again and climb out of your rut—into a more demanding position. As John Shingleton and Robert Bao explain in *From College to Career:*

> After two years on the job, you should begin thinking of a change, be it within or outside the organization. The idea is that most jobs can be mastered in, at most, two years. After that you gain very little by staying in the same job—unless you like it so much you do not wish to depart.

At that all-important two-year mark (it may be longer or shorter depending on the individual) it's time to find out how far you can advance in your own company, assuming, of course, that you want to stay on with your company. If your firm's salaries are at the industry's going rate, its benefits are good, and its reputation is fairly high, you probably will want to stay, but your company's promotional opportunities will be the deciding factor. Start exploring your own department to assess those opportunities.

You may have to look only as far as the next desk for a possible promotion. But if and when you can assume that position is another story. Talk to your boss to find out if you're the person he or she has in mind for the spot, and if you are, how long the wait will be. If your boss assures you that yes, you're the one, and yes, it'll be a matter of only months, don't take his or her word at face value. Try to get the promise in writing to protect you six months down the line when at the mention of a promise of a promotion, your boss turns to you in wide-eyed disbelief and says, "What promise?" Also consult the people in your network and your office friends for their opinion on what your boss tells you. As Cynthia, a woman on her first job, said, "My boss recently told me I'd be promoted within the year. But in talking to some people at my company, I've learned that the only way you get promoted around here is if someone leaves. And since everyone seems firmly planted, chances of my getting promoted within the next year or two are next to zero." Of course, you have to weigh such hearsay against your faith in your boss. And no one can really guarantee you anything in advance—that's one work-world reality you've learned.

What if there's no place for you to go in your department? Most career counselors will chide you, saying it's your own fault for being in such a predicament. You should never have taken a job that did not offer at least two promotion positions beyond yours, they'll lecture. But even if you possessed such career wisdom at the time you were looking for your first job, the chances are that you couldn't have used it anyway. How many job-hunters, and those setting out for their first job at that, are in situations that allow them to pick and choose from a handful of job offers?

So don't despair if there's no place to advance in your department. You'll want to talk to your boss about the possibility of recommending you for a position in another department. (Who knows, maybe he or she intends to create a new position for you within your department.) Then on your own, find out the real truth about interdepartmental moves, or else you may find yourself waiting around for a position that will never materialize. Many companies are quick to say they fill all slots from within when in reality they bring in people from the outside; so take whatever you read in the company manual on this subject with a large dose of salt. Your company contacts can probably fill you in on the realities. And if your company happens to operate an Affirmative Action (AA) program, be sure to visit the AA officer to find out about company policy regarding women.

On the basis of all the information you gather, you can intelligently decide whether you'll want to stay put in your company or go where the grass looks greener.

"I've Made a Big Mistake": Testing Career Interests

"I want to get out of auditing. It's so boring to me. I see myself moving into accounting management."

"What I learned from my first job was that I wanted to make money and couldn't do that if I stayed in publishing."

"Teaching, I found, was not all it was cracked up to be."

"Coming out of my first job, I didn't know for sure what I wanted. But I sure as heck knew what I *didn't* want."

Do any of these statements sound familiar? If you're like most women on their first job, a lot you've learned about your chosen career has startled you, disillusioned you, and maybe even made you reconsider your field of choice. But don't go around wishing someone had told you the inside information about social work before you started. ("You have no time for your clients. It's all paperwork"), or despairing that you should have been handed an exposé about the world of finance before having to stumble on the truth yourself. Your memory may fail you now, but someone probably did warn you. Some book probably did offer you all the "dirt" you wish you had heard earlier. But disregarding all you read and heard, you plunged into your field because you had to find out for yourself—which was as it should have been.

First jobs are specifically intended to test career interest. Everyone—career counselors, company presidents, guidance counselors, personnel heads, your boss, and now you—knows that. All during your career path you can double back, drop out, or turn around until you find what's right for you. But never will you feel as if you can bow out as gracefully as on your first job. You won't have to worry about getting hassled when you tell your boss, "Sorry Charlie, computer programming is just not for me." Bosses expect to hear that from a first-jobber. They've heard it before, and they'll hear it again from future first-jobbers.

Statistics corroborate this situation: most job-leaving occurs in the years twenty to twenty-four, when people are on their first or second jobs, trying careers out for size. If the field you've chosen doesn't seem right for you, ask yourself first if it is perhaps the office, the boss, or the particular specialty that's wrong for you rather than the field itself. Maybe you dislike corporate public relations but would positively thrive in a PR firm handling entertainment accounts. Try to stay open-minded about your career choice despite your initial doubts.

If you're unsure about taking a second crack at your field, talk to other people in the field. Consult those who occupy jobs similar to your own, also those from the higher ranks (positions into which you'd presumably move if you stay in your field). Get the scoop on their jobs and their firms; then compare notes. What you hear may make you want to give sales another whirl, but this time working in a different area—manufacturing, for example. Even if what you hear does convince you to leave the field, at least you'll feel you're making the right decision.

What Have You Learned?—Updating Your Résumé

The chances are you've been pretty preoccupied these days with thoughts of a new job. But have you begun to think of a campaign to move that job from the realm of your imagination to the threshold of reality? Well, you'd better get going.

The first step in any job search is to get a firm fix on what you can offer an employer. This process is called assessing your skills. Begin by asking yourself, "What have I learned in my first job?" It shouldn't take you long to come up with the answer, if you have your résumé handy—complete and updated. For a résumé serves as a capsule description of your acquired work skills and the way you put them to good use. But if you're like 99 percent of first-jobbers, you relegated your résumé to a corner of your closet the moment you signed that payroll form! (Yet another first-jobber trap you've fallen into.)

A résumé is more than a piece of paper to have at your fingertips when an ad in Sunday's classifieds catches your eye. A résumé that's constantly updated is a written self-evaluation of your work, a gauge of your progress. Remember, as we told you earlier, in the work world you can't expect much feedback from superiors as to how you're doing. That's why it's important for you to learn to assess your own growth. You have to be able to spot both your strong points and those areas in which you need to develop more proficiency. Revising your résumé at regular intervals does this for you.

A résumé charts your acquisition of skills in black and white. In the early stages of your job there may have been only one or two responsibilities in your domain. Once you established solid footing in a certain area—accounts receivable, let's say—the powers that be decided to shift you to another area, like accounts payable. And here you are today, with a large repertoire of accounting skills. If you've been updating your résumé all along, you probably have been able to edit out old skills and accomplishments that now pale in comparison to your more impressive additions (if you've just been put in charge of trust funds, it's no longer necessary to mention your expertise in accounts receivable). And it is the amount of updating you do that's the true sign of progress.

The reverse of progress—job stagnation—can be as easily detected if you keep revising your résumé. If you find you've nothing to add to—or cross out from—your résumé in six months, it's a sure sign you're not growing on the job. With your résumé as "evidence," you can then apprise your boss of the situation and talk about what action to take. (A résumé that's up to date will always be of great assistance at any career discussions you have with your boss and/or mentor.)

Now that you know the rewards of updating your résumé, retrieve your last version from the closet. To nurse yours back to health, consult *Marketing Yourself: The Catalyst Guide to Successful Résumés and Interviews* (G. P. Putnam's Sons, 1980). Once your résumé is back on its feet again, make appointments for monthly checkups (a.k.a. revising sessions).

To revise or update your résumé, you'll need to rely on more than your memory. Most people find that a note-keeping system really does the trick. Use a manila folder as your "career file," and leave it on your desk at work. Every time you inherit a new responsibility or make an important decision, write it down on a slip of paper to put in your folder. Once every month go through these notes and transfer them to your résumé. Again, *Marketing Yourself* will prove invaluable in helping you to pinpoint and emphasize newly acquired skills and achievements.

Believe it or not, updating your résumé can turn out to be a very heady experience. Working day in and out, you lose track of how much you've learned, how much you have to offer. Refreshing your résumé is a pat on the back for a job well done. Karen, a woman on her first job, admits that she looks forward to her monthly résumé-updating sessions: "Every time I go over my résumé, I think to myself, 'You know, you're pretty good.' And this feeling rubs off in my work. I go in the next day and act the outstanding professional my résumé says I am."

Career Planning

"Where do you see yourself five years from now?" In all likelihood that question was posed to you at the interview for your first job. And it probably hit you like a zinger from left field. "The nerve of them!" you thought. "How can I make a prediction? I don't know whether I'll be good at this job or even like it (and that's assuming I'll get it!). I haven't gotten my feet wet yet." No wonder so many of you felt like replying flippantly: "Oh, I'll probably be harvesting crops in the rice paddies of Malaysia!"

Well, here you are, an old pro. You don't have to untie your shoes to know your feet are wet. You've successfully undergone your initiation into the world of work. So . . . "Where do you see yourself five years from now?" Well, maybe you have an answer now—and maybe you don't. Some people get a good sense of where they fit into the wide world of work from their first job; others need a second or third job under their belts before they have an idea. Whenever the epiphany hits you—when, for instance, you wake up and know you want to be the president of a multinational corporation in five years—start taking the logical steps to reach that goal. In other words, plan your career.

If you can mark out a career course for yourself to follow, you'll be way ahead of the competition. You'd be surprised at how many people don't plan their careers. According to a spokesman for the American Management Association, roughly 90 percent of people don't; they simply drift into careers. Ninety percent! Think about it. And this figure seems to bear out the complaints most

professionals have about employees. As one training administrator said about the people at her company, "They
have a vague idea of wanting to get ahead. They want
advancement, but they don't know where." And in referring to women in general, she says, "Women, especially,
must learn to plot and plan their careers."

Why this lack of career-planning? Is it because we fear
the future and would rather live our lives according to a
"play it as it lays, one day at a time" philosophy? That
approach may explain some people's failure to plan careers.
But the majority, we believe, do not "plot and plan"
because they're confused as to what career-planning is all
about. Most people confuse it with job-hunting. To them,
career-planning is something you do to help write a résumé
or conduct a job campaign (these are the same folks who
think you prepare a résumé only when you're looking for a
job).

Career-planning is a continuous process. It's something
to think about every day of your working life, not something to forget about once you land a job. Career-planning
involves setting goals for yourself (after two years: assistant
vice president; after four more years: senior vice-president).
And keeping these goals in mind, it means availing yourself
of opportunities at work that can help you reach them.
Judith Warner, a training administrator, explains that "you
have to see yourself functioning as a means to an end. You
have to realize that you use one situation to get to another.
You can't go into a job and say, 'I'm going to do this job as
best I can forever.' Rather, start thinking, What skills can I
gain from this that can help me move to another area?"

And to make sure the skills you amass are the right
ones, fashion your career path after someone you know
who has already taken that same path. According to Lolita
Schalleck, director of career development programs for
women at CBS, this method is a surefire way of successfully
planning your career:

It's much easier to plan down than it is to plan up. Ask yourself: How many people do I know in the position I eventually want? How long have they been there? Where have they come from? Let's say I want to be a director of marketing and I know five directors of marketing. They all started as a marketing analyst, then the next job was senior analyst, and then the next job was manager, and 3½ years later they were working as the assistant to the director. Meantime they had gone back to school and gotten their MBA's. If I could put together a package similar to that, including those same jobs, chances are I'd get the position I want.

"That sounds smart," you say, "but I'm not the kind of person who can follow such a structured path, and it sounds pretty rigid." It is and it isn't. The whole idea behind planning ahead is to provide yourself with a framework to reach your career goals. How you assemble that framework is up to you For instance, you may choose to attain your goals at a faster or a slower pace. Maybe you'll want time off built into that framework to raise a child or travel. Maybe you'll want to earn that advanced degree in less than two years. And, most important, you have to realize that your goals might very well change, so your career plans should be flexible enough to allow that to happen. Career counselor Barbara Holt thinks that "there should be some sense of that's the direction I want to go in, that's what I think is the ideal a few years out, and here are some of the ways I can build the bridge *backward* from there to where I am."

And always, always keep your options open. You may discover a brand-new career along the way, the one that was really meant for you. "I don't think you should have to feel that what you've decided at 22 is it for life," says Kathleen Conway, who was an elementary school teacher before joining New York Life Insurance as a supervisor of training programs. "Because if you have that attitude, you can close

yourself off to a lot of things. If I had said teaching is it—
there are no other options—I don't think I'd have ended up
here and have been so happy." (Happiness . . . your career
should contribute to yours.)

School Days

Whether it's a college seminar in "Decision Systems for
Corporate Strategic Planning" or an in-house crash course
in the "Basics of Typography," sooner or later you'll be
cracking those textbooks (and you thought you'd never
open another one again!). It may be that you're expected to
acquire certain technical knowledge before you can assume
the next promotional position. Or that you'll have to pick
up a course on theory to complement the "nuts and bolts"
education you receive at work.

For whatever reason you seek further training, taking
courses lets your boss and company know you're serious
about getting ahead. That's why the M.B.A. is today's most
sought-after degree. "One of the things an M.B.A. says to
the world is that I'm committed to business for the rest of
my life, that I will retire like everyone else at age 65," notes
CBS's Lolita Schalleck. She feels that women are in sore
need of gaining professional legitimacy in business and an
M.B.A. is one of the best ways of achieving it.

The pleasant part about going back to school at this
stage of the game is that your company very often pays most
if not all of your tuition bills. A recent study conducted by
AT&T shows that 93 percent of large firms operate some
form of tuition program for courses that are related to
work. (And if you're employed by a small concern without
such a program, you're eligible to take educational expenses
as a job-related tax deduction.) Fortunately, most firms
with tuition aid programs do not require you to be employed for a long period of time before you qualify (a great

boon if you've just started your first job). Nor do they stipulate that you must remain in their employ after you finish your course or degree.

The only catch to tuition programs is that you're usually reimbursed *after* you finish a course. Stockpile some savings before enrolling so you won't get caught in a financial crunch. If your company doesn't have a tuition program and you're considering graduate school, inquire about various federal and state grants and loan programs at your college's financial aid office. Also, many professional associations and unions sponsor scholarships for their members. Find out if yours do.

If it is the graduate school route for you, be forewarned that working full time and going to school is no picnic. Picture yourself working all day, coming home tense and exhausted, racing off to class, mustering up mental alertness once there, then returning home dead tired to study for the next class's lesson. Repeat that scene three nights a week, fourteen weeks a semester. For that duration you can pretty much kiss your social life, and friends, and family goodbye. Working and going to school can be grueling, no doubt about it. But the temporary hardship you'll endure is an investment in the future, one you'll never regret having made.

COLLECTING CREDENTIALS

If you don't already have one, start a career file for yourself. Clean out that bottom drawer and put it to better use. The important papers you save now may mean dollars earned in the future. They will document your accomplishments when it's time to look for a new job, or to ask for a raise. Here are things you positively must save:

- Anything you've helped prepare, whether by researching, writing, designing, printing, etc. This includes correspondence, memoranda, reports, brochures, sales charts, publications, proposals, and the like.

- Letters of commendation from teachers, bosses, clients, customers, coworkers, and peers. (If a performance interview is strictly verbal—the boss simply says you're doing a great job—ask him/her to put it in writing "so that you can look at it and cheer yourself up on days when it seems as if nothing is going right.")

- Diplomas or certificates of graduation/completion of courses, classes, workshops, seminars, training programs, etc. Similarly, save programs from meetings where you've been a panelist or speaker, or syllabi and summaries of participants' evaluations from classes you've taught. (When deciding whether to participate in such activities or not, as a learner or teacher, give a thought to how they'll look on your résumé. They can indicate to employers that you're keeping yourself up to date in your field, developing new skills, widening your area of experience/expertise, and becoming known by people in your field.)

- Newspaper clippings in which you've been quoted, or that describe activities you've been involved in.

- Any creative work that you've done, or plans that you've developed. These might be in the form of memos, proposals, evaluations, or finished projects.

MOVING ON

14

ALL GOOD THINGS come to an end. And all not-so-good things too. Whether your first job was good or merely so-so, the time will come when you and your job must go your separate ways.

But how will I be able to recognize when this time comes, you ask. Well, it won't reveal itself to you in a dream or a divine revelation. Nor will your boss knock on your cubicle window and say, "Hey kid, the jig's up!"

What will start to happen, though, is that you'll begin feeling terribly dissatisfied with your job. And this dissatisfaction usually manifests itself in any of these telltale signs:

- You start coming in late.

- You start leaving early.

- You're taking a lot of sick days as "mental health" days.

- You're having fewer arguments with your boss and coworkers because issues at work suddenly don't seem worth fighting over, or you're having more fights with

255

the folks at work because a good brawl is the only on-the-job stimulation around.

- You don't talk about your job anymore to your friends, or work is all you talk about, and as a result your friends have stopped seeing you.

The kind of job dissatisfaction we're talking about stems from a lack of challenge on the job. You've learned all there is to learn; the number of new areas you can be exposed to has dwindled to zero. You feel stifled and unfulfilled. As we discussed earlier, you'll probably reach this point after two years. But every job is different. Yours may turn out to be so limiting that you will have exhausted its possibilities within a year. On the other hand, you may have to stick around three or four years before you can confidently say, "I've learned it all and done it all."

Is It Time to Quit?

But when you're feeling confident that the time has come for you to clean out your desk, allow yourself to play the devil's advocate. Ask yourself, "Am I perhaps leaving too soon?" For, as one woman supervisor acknowledged, "Most of us are tempted far before the point when we should leave." Remember, taking your leave later than you should won't necessarily set your career back, but leaving prematurely may put you at a disadvantage. So even if your workplace resembles a turn-of-the-century sweatshop and your boss makes Scrooge look like Santa Claus, if there's something yet to learn, something worth staying on for at your job, stick it out.

And be careful not to confuse any job dissatisfaction you may experience with plain old itchiness that hits at regular intervals. Take an extended weekend or a vacation, usually the quickest cure for the occasional despair that afflicts most workers. But if you're still feeling disgruntled once you return, it probably is honest-to-God job dissatisfaction that's been plaguing you after all. So get packing.

The actual leavetaking of a job, though, is easier said than done. One woman we know stayed on her first job for nine years, simply because she didn't have the gumption to leave. "I had grown so comfortable in my job," she says, "that I was afraid and reluctant to make any move."

A job can easily turn into a security blanket for you. You know the people there, you know what's required of you. Why give up what you know for what you don't know?

For your personal growth and fulfillment, that's why. You may be up to your ears already with all this talk about growth and fulfillment. But we wouldn't be making such a fuss about it if it weren't important. And it is. More important than the circle of friends you have at the office. Important enough for you to take a risk, which is what leaving a job is all about. And risk-taking is frightening, no doubt about it. One woman we spoke to describes how she dealt with her dread of changing jobs:

> You have to decide which is the greater feeling for you—the feeling of rank boredom (if you stay on at your present job), or the feeling of being frightened (if you choose to leave it). For me, it was the feeling of being frightened. I then had to figure out what I was going to do with this feeling. The answer I came up with was to simply do what I feared, to leave my old job and take on a new one.

You may have your own system of ridding yourself of fear; use it. (We've been told that holding yourself erect and whistling a happy tune works.) After you conquer your fear, start working on your guilt feelings. For good old guilt is the number-two reason why most people postpone leaving their jobs. And the guilt you're probably going through about leaving your first job is one of the heftiest loads you'll ever carry in your career lifetime. "Oh, everyone's been so nice to me," you're thinking. "My boss has taught me everything she knows. How can I run out on her?" Easily. Believe us, bosses are aware of the risks of training a person on her first job. It was sure to have crossed your boss's mind that one day you may take what she's taught you and fly off. It's up to you now to rid yourself of your indentured slave mentality.

You didn't sign a contract when you were hired, promising you'd stay on seven years and a day. "You have to realize you have a base to stand on too," advises Marilyn, a woman who's had a number of jobs and guilt trips to match. "So you received a lot from your employer, but you gave a lot in return. You did your work, just like any other employee. You really don't owe your boss a thing, certainly not your staying on any longer." If you can take these words to heart, you'll find leavetaking to be easy for you this first time, and even easier the second and third time around.

Job-Hunting

Job-hunting, we must admit, is not the most ennobling of experiences. Remember how it was for you the first time? Interviewers reduced you to Jell-O; mailboxes held only rejection in the form of form letters. But once you accustomed yourself to the futility of ever finding a job, and you did, recall how daring you became? You answered ads for "ten-year veterans in the field"; you phoned that member of the board of IBM to talk her into giving you a job.

You may be relieved to learn that you won't have to experience such desperation when you start looking for your second position. Why? Before now you were confronting the *Catch-22* mentality that operates in the business world: "To get hired, you need experience; to get experience, you need to be hired." Well, you defeated that vicious circle—you were hired, you've gained experience. As a result, looking for a job this time around will probably be a lot shorter, and a lot less painful.

And think of it, you're in the privileged position of looking for a job while on a job—a far more comfortable existence than the people in those unemployment lines lead. Ah, but you probably think you don't *have* it so good. "I'd rather quit tomorrow and start looking," you say. Don't you dare. We repeat, *Don't.* For one reason, your value increases in the job market if you're holding down a job; you become a wanted "property." You see, having a job does a lot for your image. You're regarded by prospective employers as a woman who's making a conscious career move, someone who knows what she's about. And you can take advantage of this image and play it for all it's worth.

And then there are those obvious benefits of looking while on a job—time and money. Take time, for instance. Even though you have glowing credentials, the chances are you're not going to be snapped up by an employer as soon as you throw your hat (résumé) into the ring. On the average, it takes about three months for a person to land a good job (and by that we mean the job of your choice). And then there's the matter of money. If you were to leave your job now to look for another, think how life would be without that paycheck coming in every week. You wouldn't want to put yourself in a situation in which you'd have to grab the first job that came your way out of financial necessity. So stay put while you're looking.

Where do you start to job hunt? The majority of "good" jobs are rarely advertised. Rather, they're filled through an informal network, an underground of people tapping talented eligibles in the field. If you've been out mingling as you should have been (see Chapter 10 on "networking"), you are already plugged into that network. Call the contacts you have at your disposal and invite them out to lunch or drinks. Let them know that though you're relatively happy where you are now (again, always play it cool), you're starting to keep an eye out for a new position. If they don't know of any openings offhand, they might supply you with the names of other people who may know. And so your list of contacts grows.

Even if you've been in a cocoon for the past few months and don't know a single soul to ask, you can quickly recruit a few. Start drawing up a list of all the people you've spoken to outside your company in the past few months. And we mean *everyone:* from the stationery supply salesman to a leading client's secretary, to the leading client herself, to friends and family. Then just shed your embarrassment and give these people a call. You'll be pleasantly surprised at their willingness to help you.

You may be dead set on leaving your company, but stop by at Personnel and check the job postings anyway. Something listed there could change your mind. If you have a good relationship with one of the Personnel counselors, talk to him or her. Personnel staffs can usually be trusted to keep your job-hunting intents in confidence. Also, speak to members of your company's network. Aside from knowing of in-house openings, they may cue you in to some outside ones as well.

Also, stop by your local library and discover the wealth of job-hunting information sources awaiting you there (college libraries are your best bet, but local public libraries have facilities to help in many cases also). Industrial directories can supply you with names and addresses and basic data on companies in your field. Check trade magazines and newsletters to see which companies are current forerunners in the field, and therefore the ones most likely to be hiring. (Ideally, you should have gotten your name on the magazine routing list at work and have been keeping abreast of this information all along.) You'll want to jot down names of leading executives from these sources to send résumés.

As for the actual on-the-job search, proceed with discretion. Try to schedule interviews during your lunch hour or after five. Otherwise, plan on taking days off from work or calling in sick to go on interviews. If you have to call a prospective employer during the day, do it from a pay phone, not at your desk. In much the same way, resist the temptation to photocopy your covering letters in the office; take a walk to a local copying place instead.

You shouldn't include your office phone number on your résumé. Most employers will drop you a short letter if they wish to see you. An answering service is worth the cost—it pays off when you get that job you were working for through one of the calls. And as much as you'd like to, don't breathe a word about what you're doing to your colleagues; you just never know how it could backfire on you. As for the possibility of a potential employer calling your boss for a reference, relax. They usually don't call for a character check until you have the job neatly sewn up.

Are you considering a job for which you'd have to relocate? Think of how your life will be affected by such a move. How do you feel about being thirty miles from the nearest Chinese restaurant, or breathing city pollution instead of fresh air, or being deprived of friends and family? Things you may have never given a second thought to must be considered when deciding whether or not to relocate.

Our advice: don't accept a job in a new area until you've stayed there for at least a short time. It's a good idea to take a week's vacation to investigate the surroundings. You'll want to explore the streets and parks, go apartment-hunting, find out about local transportation, check the prices of food and clothing, and see what the social and entertainment scene is like. You'll then be able to put together a list of the pluses and minuses of moving to that area, and decide whether it'll be worth your while to relocate. Let's say an out-of-town job offers you more money, but in visiting the city you've found the cost of living to be sky-high. Therefore your reason for possibly relocating—for financial gain—is no longer valid.

Changing locales is a serious step to take. Give yourself enough time to consider all the various ramifications of a move, and you'll come up with an intelligent decision—one that's right for you.

What to Look for in Your Next Job

When you were looking for your first job, you probably had only two questions to pose to any of your interviewers: "How much does the job pay?" and "When can I start?"

You were young and innocent then, and ignorant. Fortunately, you've picked up a lot of business "smarts" since. In going for your second job, you know now that it should offer you more than a good salary. You'll be examining a potential job for these three basic requirements: that it offers you promotional opportunities; that it will teach you new skills; and that it will fulfill your personal job needs.

Let's examine these criteria, starting with the importance of finding a job with good promotional chances. You may have wished you had discussed this topic in greater detail when you went looking for your first job. For if you had, you would have perhaps found a first job that naturally gave way to a second job. But you were not alone in failing to inquire about promotions. Most job-hunters simply assume that promotion possibilities are built into every job, that there always is a place for one to go, and never think to ask. Promotional possibilities vary from company to company and from job to job. So never assume that they exist.

Ask. Here is a sampling of questions on this topic you'll want to take with you on an interview:

How many people are in the department?
What do they do?
Were they all promoted within the department?
How long does it take for a person to be promoted in this department?
Was the person whose job you'd be assuming promoted in the department? If not, where did he or she go?
What's required of an employee before he or she gets promoted?
Is it possible to be promoted across department lines?

The next item to discuss at an interview is whether the job will enable you to learn new skills. Gaining additional skills is, of course, a necessity for your career growth and development. If you translated someone else's designs into blueprints, perhaps it's time you learned to design; if you supervised just one person on your first go-around, you should be looking for a position allowing you to manage a group.

The best way to find out if a job will provide you with the skills you're after is to ask the interviewer for a job description, preferably in writing. Never assume you know what a job is all about just from its title. With a job description, you'll be able to tell if the job has, indeed, new terrain to explore. Then be sure to ask who the person is who will be guiding you along that terrain, and to meet that person. If your interviewer tells you you'll be learning on your own, you should be somewhat cautious. Such an answer is usually a sign that there's not much to learn. Try to discover as many job details as you can.

Personnel administrator Jane Nemke offers the following good advice: "Take time to interview the company and be aware of what your potential boss is like and whether he or she will be willing to spend the time in training you. My own career and advancement seem to be directly related to the quality of boss I've had.

"One thing you can do is to try to get hold of some people who worked for your potential boss. Talk with them informally about what this person is like, what it's like to work for him or her. Another thing I rely on is my gut feeling—you can tell when you're speaking with someone whether or not you're going to have a rapport with him or her."

Don't forget to find out if a job will satisfy your personal job needs. What do we mean by job needs? Everyone approaches his/her work in a certain way, or functions best under specific conditions. You, for instance, may require total peace and quiet to get anything done. The next person may thrive when placed alongside coworkers who keep up a constant banter. You may think such needs are incidental; it's more important, you say, to find a position that offers you new skills and opportunities for advancement. But if your personal job requirements aren't being met, who's to say you'll stay long enough to get promoted?

So to help you to identify your personal jobs needs, we've put together a checklist of some of the most common ones. Check off those that apply to you.

☐ You like to work independently.
☐ You need strict supervision.

☐ You're willing to work late hours or weekends for your job.
☐ You refuse to put in a minute past your eight hours.

☐ You need to work away from others.
☐ You work best surrounded by coworkers.

☐ You like to juggle assignments.
☐ You'd rather handle one project at a time.

☐ You need time to goof off.
☐ You like it when your nose is to the grindstone seven hours a day.

☐ You thrive under deadline pressure.
☐ You'd rather set your own working pace.

☐ You like feeling indispensable.
☐ You'd rather not be the only person who knows how to do everything that needs to get done.

How do you talk about these needs when you're in an interview? With a great deal of caution. Many of these needs can be misconstrued as signs of unprofessional behavior by an interviewer. So if you checked off that you'd rather be dispensable than indispensable or that you need goofing-off time, phrase your statements in the converse. Instead of saying, "I refuse to work overtime," ask, "How much overtime is there?" This way you come across as someone who anticipates overtime and will readily accept it—someone who clearly is a professional. Don't worry if you sound misleading. All you're after is information, and phrasing your questions in the way we suggest will provide you with all the facts. Once you have them, you can then decide if you want to enter into such a situation.

Of course, finding a job that fulfills all your job needs is a rarity. So is finding one that precisely fulfills all three of your criteria. Maybe you'll come across a job that offers good promotion possibilities, is a little weak in the new-skills department, and is satisfactory with regard to your job needs. Or maybe you'll interview for a job whose strongest selling point is in the new-skills area. Make your choice after carefully weighing all these factors.

As long as you actively participate in interviews by asking questions, you'll come away with all the information you need to intelligently choose your second job.

Testing, Testing . . .

Job-hoppers used to be scorned members of our society. The longer your résumé, the more suspicion you drew from the staid and stable working public. You were considered uncommitted, irresponsible, and flighty.

That's not the situation anymore. Job-hopping has not only become respectable, it is now considered *de rigueur* for anyone who wants to get ahead. One woman manager sums up the current opinion on job-hopping: "Until you've gotten some good experience, you've got to make a few jumps to get ahead." Nowadays those who don't hop are looked upon as odd. "What's wrong with Sally? She's been on that same job for nearly four years" is the line you're most likely to hear.

This attitude is quite different from the one our parents had. On embarking on their first jobs, they were told, "Stick with your company, it's a good one." They followed that advice, and gold watches commemorating forty years of service were theirs. No gold watches, we're afraid, for this current generation of workers. And it's not that people are trying out five or six different companies in search of a "good one." A lot of "good ones" out there employ a lot of people. Nowadays job-hopping is regarded as the quickest way to advance professionally. By job-hopping, *you* "promote" yourself to the next position (or even higher) at another company.

But job-hopping has its risks. You have to be sure that the position you hop to will offer you real growth or advancement. Otherwise you'll only have a long list of jobs to show for yourself. One look at that "list," and a prospective employer will think, "She can't hold down a job. What is the likelihood of her keeping this one?"

So before you accept a new position anywhere, see that the job offers either an increase in responsibility and salary or the chance to learn new skills. Don't be taken in by fancy titles, either. Ask for a complete job description so you can tell whether you're being offered a position of substance.

And don't give job-hopping a whirl until you've had your fill of your first job. Even if everyone else seems to be "doing it," don't feel as if you must join them. "I was really getting paranoid there for a while," says Carol, a woman on her first job in a manufacturing firm. "Friends of mine were telling me that in order to go places you shouldn't stay long at any job, even your first. One friend left her first job after four months." Most first jobs have a lot to offer you, surely more than four months' worth! And remember, you don't have to clock yourself to anyone's career timetable.

If after your first job you're still unsure about what you want to do, you may want to engage in an exploratory type of job-hopping by which you investigate different career fields. Granted, this is not easy to do. You'll have to be able to sit down and convince an employer you have work skills that are "translatable" if, let's say, you're going from a job in computer programming to one in public relations. And if you opt for this sort of hopping, be prepared for low salaries. You'll be coming without clear-cut experience in a new area and will probably be slotted to beginning, poor-paying positions. Such a sacrifice is worth it, though, when you think of the exposure in different career fields you'll be getting. One of those fields is bound to suit you.

How long should you job-hop? Try not to make a career out of it. The aim of job-hopping is ultimately to find a place to put down roots. And that should come when you find a job or a company that you feel offers you the best opportunities. Only you can be the judge of that.

Leaving with Tact

Hooray, you've landed your second job. You're ready to bound into your boss's office, announce the good news, clear out your desk, and grab the next plane to Tobago for a quickie vacation.

Sorry, but you just can't kiss and run. That may be the way you end affairs of the heart, but business affairs are another story. In the work world, you'll be remembered more for how you left a job than for what you did prior to leaving. So to make your leave-taking memorable, it's imperative that you follow a certain etiquette.

Let your boss know of your planned departure as soon as you know. Resist the temptation to tell any of your coworkers; the least you owe your boss is that he or she hears the news first from you. The standard rule of thumb is to give an employer two weeks' notice. But if you can safely predict that you'll be needed a bit longer to train your successor, ask your new employer possibly to postpone your starting date for another week. Your new employer will undoubtedly agree to this and be very impressed by your dedication and conscientiousness; they'll realize you'd probably do the same for them one day. Needless to say, your old employer will be very grateful that you can stay on a while longer, and will supply you with glowing references for doing so.

How do you break the news to your boss? Whether your relationship with your boss has been close, and he or she through career discussions has anticipated your leaving, or whether the relationship has been cool and distant and the news will come as a real surprise, the method of breaking that news is the same. Tell your boss you're leaving because you've learned all you could there and are moving on to the next logical step (if your new boss is going to call your old one for references, it's best to inform him or her just where you're going). Even if you're leaving because you disliked the work or couldn't get along with your boss, use the same line: you are leaving to advance your career to the next step. And a little flattery and gratitude can do you no harm on parting. Thank your boss for his or her patience with you as you learned the ropes, and for his or her attempts at making life at work as painless and pleasurable as possible. In short, look at the good side and try to paint a rosy picture of your time there.

But that's being hypocritical, you say. You want to tell your boss your true feelings, every one of them! Sure, we all have a script ready in our head for the time we say adieu: "I'm busting out of this hellish place at last, boss. The work was intolerable, my coworkers are a bunch of idiots, and you, dear boss, have brought new meaning to the Peter Principle. Incompetence suits you well."

When you think about it, delivering such a speech won't change the way your boss acts. Nor will it improve the standard of working, if it has been that poor, for your successors. Hurling invectives will only lower your esteem in your boss's eyes forever more. And you never know when you might need another reference or another job from him or her again. So don't burn your bridges by being nasty in the name of truth.

Your boss will probably fill you in on your company's specific procedures for leave-taking. Many firms require you to draw up a formal letter of resignation. Usually all that's necessary is a brief "This letter is to inform you of my resignation from your employment effective June 1, 1981." You'll want to visit your company's personnel department to find out about getting compensated for any unused vacation time, and whether you'll still be covered by your old health insurance plans until you're accepted into your new company's plans.

During your "final days" you'll want to tie up all loose ends. Clear out old files, bring all your notes up to date, draw up memos on the status of all your projects, and distribute any unfinished work. Getting your house in order may require working extra hours. So put in an evening or two; skip a lunch hour here and there. Regard your leave-taking as a time for final sacrifices, not new-found liberties like coming in late or taking three-hour lunches.

As for training a new person, we recommend you focus your energies on instructing her to perform the work. Forget about giving her the lowdown on your coworkers, your boss, and the company in general. That'll be part of her on-the-job training. You wouldn't want to deprive her of such a learning experience, would you? Then again, maybe she won't see things in the same light as you did. She has to find out for herself.

We can't promise you that your last few weeks at your first job will be pleasant. Very few workers receive a jubilant going-away. If anything, expect the cold-shoulder treatment. Why? It's ridiculous to assume that everyone will share in your happiness. Your boss, for instance, might be upset at having to find your replacement. And your co-workers, though genuinely sorry to see you go, may also feel jealous and angry. To them, the message implicit in your leaving is as follows: "This place and this job might be good enough for you, but not for me." Perhaps on your leave-taking you'll be the recipient of a round of hand-shakes and best wishes. But if up to the day you walk out that door all you do get is a cold shoulder, try to remain your usual friendly self. Make an effort to understand the reasons why your boss and coworkers are reacting as they are.

Leaving with tact is yet another test of handling yourself professionally. And it is the last test of what was essentially a testing experience—your first job.

WHAT TO DO WHEN YOU'RE FIRED OR LAID OFF

Though you may think it will never happen to you, getting fired or laid off is always a possibility, even on your first job. Losing your job is one of those work realities you should mentally prepare for . . . just in case.

If you have the misfortune of learning that your first job is ending sooner than you anticipated, don't rush off to the welcoming arms of the nearest graduate school, convinced you're a failure in the business world. You're not a failure, just a statistic—thousands of people lose their jobs every day. So try to maintain a healthy attitude about the whole situation. One man we spoke to had an exceedingly refreshing outlook on getting fired: "It's not the worst thing in the world if I were to be fired. It would be worse if someone broke into my home and stole all my possessions, or if all my friends left me. That I would feel bad about."

Once you get your attitude adjusted, it's time to make some financial provisions for your period of unemployment. Before leaving your company, find out from Personnel how long you'll be covered by the medical insurance plan. You may then want to call a few insurance companies and inquire about their individual medical plans. Being sick and unemployed and uninsured is a triple threat you don't want to risk. Next on your agenda is a stop at your state's unemployment office to see if you can sign up for benefits. Each state administers its own program and eligibility requirements, and benefits do vary. But if you do qualify, you can count on getting approximately 50 percent of your old wages for about twenty-six weeks. Anyway, you should have money set aside in the bank for such an emergency (three months of your salary is a good sum). Knowing you have cash funds to tide you over for a while will let you sleep more soundly at night.

Rather than rushing off the day after you get your pink slip to find your second job, you'll be better off taking a few days to calm down, quiet your nerves, and most of all, to put your last job in perspective. Start by asking yourself, why is it that you are what you are—jobless? If you were laid off, the answer is easy enough: your company may have had a bad year, or perhaps your division was eliminated in a streamlining campaign. In a layoff, circumstances are clearly out of your control. Not so if you're fired. Most workers are either partly or totally responsible for their getting fired. It may be a bitter pill for you to swallow, but you must confront the real truth behind your firing. Otherwise you may find yourself in the same situation again and again, and pretty soon you'll have a foot-high stack of pink slips to show for yourself.

So think hard. We'll offer some assistance. If you've had the dubious distinction of getting fired from your first job, it probably was because you were the wrong person for the job. Like most people on their first job, you accepted the first offer you received, right? That was not the wisest thing to do, but what did you know back then, anyway? Maybe you were an art major who took a position in a legal firm. It wasn't long before you grew frustrated proofreading law briefs and torts all day and your attitude began to reflect in your work, which grew to be slipshod. Your superiors noticed (they're always watching, you know) and gave you the axe. It's not that you were a failure at work. A law office just wasn't the right work environment for you. Now, in retrospect, you realize you would have been better off holding out till you found a job in a museum, or art gallery, or a company that in some way was related to art. Well, you've another chance now to find the right job. A fresh start can be yours.

Being unemployed is a good experience in that it forces you to examine your career goals, to think about what you want to do and where you want to do it. Says Rita, a woman who was fired from her first job: "Getting fired was one of the best things that ever happened to me; I sent my boss a thank-you letter for doing it! I was unhappy at my job but probably would have stayed on, just grinding away. Losing my job made me realize that I was not suited for administrative work. I'm a creative type, and I've found a job now where I can use my talents." You too during your temporary joblessness should be putting your career in order, thinking of what you want from your next job. Then when you're ready, go after your "dream job."

A FEW WORDS ON MAKING IT

15

SUCCESS. It's a concept that you've lived with all your life. Time and time again it was drummed into your head—by your teachers, parents, friends, even your swimming coach—succeed at *whatever* you set out to do. And everyone was always "measuring" your degree of success, giving you A's or F's, raising your allowance for a good report card, or making you stay after school to do extra work. Unconsciously, perhaps, you learned to live with that pressure to succeed—whether it was to pass a trig test or be accepted into college.

And now the pressure on you to succeed seems greater than ever before. In your new role of working woman, you're making your way in what has been traditionally a man's turf. Friends, colleagues, even the media are all rooting for (requiring?) you to leave your mark in that world; so much so that you're worried that you'll disappoint them all—and also yourself. And in the process, you'll be letting down all womankind.

"Now there's so much emphasis on succeeding at your job," said Kathy, a first-jobber, "that it's hard to separate yourself from your job. If something bad happens at work, I go home and feel less worthwhile. I don't know if it is because I'm reading so much about 'superwomen.' If I had a bad day and go home and the house is messy, I feel as if I'm not doing *that* well either."

In every magazine, on every television talk show, you see women who are noted corporate heads, celebrated defense attorneys, rich entrepreneurs, journalistic geniuses, and you think to yourself, "Why can't I be like them or have what they have?!" Once gender distinguished you from those media types, and you could console yourself by saying, "Sure they're successful—they're men. The opportunities they had just aren't available to women." So much for excuses. Those opportunities denied to your mother and grandmother are now yours for the taking. So why is it you're not the person on the TV screen, or featured in the latest women's magazine? Why isn't your wall covered by awards? "Why am *I* not successful?" you ask.

Stop. Don't be fooled into thinking that other people's definitions of success are your own. "Success" is quite a nebulous word, meaning different things to different people. Some people measure it in terms of job satisfaction, others in terms of power, prestige, or money. For still others, fame and fortune constitute the *entire* definition. For most of us, success comes to mean a combination of all these characteristics.

What is success?

"Having a male secretary! I've always been dying to say to someone, 'Well, my secretary Joe was taking my notes, and he's lost them!' "

"First thing is liking my work; second thing, getting my way—that's my definition of power. Third thing would be having influence on others, a sense of significance that my work matters, it's important—that it's worthwhile and actually benefits people."

"Salaries and promotions, I think, are really not the

primary evidence of success. You can be getting two-thou-
sand-dollar raises every year, but if you hate what you
do . . . ! In that instance, I don't think you're successful—just
successful in making more money."

"Success is relative. If I was doing the same thing ten
years from now, I wouldn't consider myself successful. I think
at *this* stage of my life I am somewhat successful because I've
finally found something that I basically enjoy doing—and I
get paid! I guess I have a degree of it."

However you come to define success for yourself—take
it one step at a time. It's easy to become impatient. Having
gotten a taste of the real world, you find that there's so
much you want *now*. It's a natural reaction of a person on
her/his first job; it seems as if you've put in an interminable
amount of time reaching point A, and now you're ready and
anxious to tackle points B, C, and D all at once. You've
seen the president of your company in action and know
beyond the shadow of a doubt that you could easily step
into his or her shoes tomorrow. Maybe. Probably not. Just
remember that that man or woman has spent many years
learning to get to the top. Along the way he or she paid a lot
of dues and made some tradeoffs. Maybe you will too. But
in the meantime, you'll have to learn to bide your time with
all the other first-jobbers out there and make the best of
each opportunity as it comes along.

In conducting the interviews for this book, we found one
component that was included in everyone's definition of
success: job satisfaction—a sense of liking what you do. Job
satisfaction, said our interviewees, is as important as getting
a high salary or professional prestige. Moreover, they told
us, there's no guarantee that you will attain fame and
fortune, but job satisfaction is pretty much within everyone's grasp. "I don't care what you do," said one first-
jobber. "You can be a brain surgeon, a mechanic, or an
executive—if *you're* happy with what you're doing, I think

you are a success. Because if you feel good about your work, you'll feel good about yourself."

You can be a success at many stages of your career. There is really no ultimate pinnacle of achievement for anyone—there's always another step you can take, another direction to turn. Take time to "savor" each step of the journey; have a little fun along the way.

Next time you're confronted with all these "supermen/women," don't be too hard on yourself. There's no reason not to include your name in the league of the successful. Each night you go home feeling good about yourself, that's a success. Each time you learn a new skill or master a new job, you're a success. And yes, each time you get a raise or a promotion, you're a success too. Write your own definitions. In the end, you will be the only *real* judge of your accomplishments.

Good luck!

BIBLIOGRAPHY/
SUGGESTED READING

General Job-Hunting/Career-Advancement Skills

Abarbanel, Karin, and Gonnie McClung Siegel. *Women's Work Book*. New York: Praeger, 1975.

Bird, Caroline. *Everything a Woman Needs to Know to Get Paid What She's Worth*. New York: McKay, 1973.

Bolles, Richard N. *What Color Is Your Parachute?* (rev. ed.). Berkeley: Ten Speed Press, 1979.

Catalyst. *Marketing Yourself: The Catalyst Women's Guide to Successful Resumes and Interviews*. New York: Putnam, 1980.

Catalyst. *What to Do with the Rest of Your Life: The Catalyst Career Guide for Women in the '80s*. New York: Simon and Schuster, 1980.

Crain, Sharie, and Phillip T. Drotning. *Taking Stock: A Woman's Guide to Corporate Success*. Chicago: Contemporary Books, 1977.

DuBrin, Andrew J. *Survival in the Office: How to Move Ahead or Hang On*. New York: Van Nostrand Reinhold, 1977.

Figler, Howard. *The Complete Job-Search Handbook*. New York: Holt, Rinehart & Winston, 1979.

Fox, Marcia R. *Put Your Degree to Work*. New York: Norton, 1979.

Friedman, Sande, and Lois C. Schwartz. *No Experience Necessary: A Guide to Employment for the Female Liberal Arts Graduate.* New York: Dell, 1971.

Goldfein, Donna. *Everywoman's Guide to Travel.* Millbrae, Cal.: Les Femmes Pub., 1977.

Halcomb, Ruth. *Women Making It: Patterns and Profiles of Success.* New York: Atheneum, 1979.

Harragan, Betty Lehan. *Games Mother Never Taught You.* New York: Warner Books, 1978.

Higginson, Margaret V., and Thomas L. Quick. *The Ambitious Woman's Guide to a Successful Career.* New York: American Management Association, 1975.

Irish, Richard K. *Go Hire Yourself an Employer.* Garden City, N.Y.: Anchor Press, 1978.

Kanter, Rosabeth Moss. *Men and Women of the Corporation.* New York: Basic Books, 1979.

Keene, Roland, ed., *Work and the College Student: Proceedings.* Carbondale, Ill.: Southern Illinois University Press, 1976.

Moldafsky, Annie. *Welcome to the Real World: A Guide to Making Your First Personal, Financial, and Career Decisions.* Garden City, N.Y.: Doubleday, 1979.

Moore, Charles Guy. *The Career Game* (rev. ed.). New York: National Institute of Career Planning, 1978.

Pogrebin, Letty Cottin. *Getting Yours.* New York: Avon, 1976.

Pogrebin, Letty Cottin. *How to Make It in a Man's World.* Garden City, N.Y.: Doubleday, 1970.

Scheele, Adele M. *Skills for Success.* New York: William Morrow and Co., Inc., 1979

Schoenberg, Robert J. *The Art of Being a Boss: Inside Intelligence from Top-Level Business Leaders and Young Executives on the Move.* New York: Lippincott, 1978.

Shingleton, John D. and Robert Bao. *College to Career,*

Finding Yourself in the Job Market. New York: McGraw-Hill, 1977.

Steele, Addison. *Upward Nobility: How to Win the Rat Race Without Becoming a Rat*. New York: Times Books, 1978.

Sweet, Donald H. *The Job Hunter's Manual*. Reading, Mass.: Addison-Wesley, 1975.

Townsend, Robert C. *Up the Organization*. New York: Knopf, 1970.

Ward, Lewis B., and Anthony Athos. *Student Expectations of Corporate Life: Implications for Management Recruiting*. Boston: Harvard Business School, Division of Research, 1972.

Williams, Marcille. *The New Executive Woman*. Radnor, Pa.: Chilton, 1977.

Sexual Harassment

Farley, Lin. *Sexual Shakedown: The Sexual Harassment of Women on the Job*. New York: McGraw-Hill, 1978.

MacKinnon, Catharine A. *Sexual Harassment of Working Women: A Case of Sex Discrimination*. New Haven, Conn.: Yale University Press, 1979.

Personal Finances

Ahern, Dee Dee. *The Economics of Being a Woman*. New York: Macmillan, 1976.

Auerbach, Sylvia. *A Woman's Book of Money: A Guide to Financial Independence*. Garden City, N.Y.: Dolphin Books, 1976.

Groza, Mavis Arthur. *Everywoman's Guide to Financial Independence*. Millbrae, Cal.: Les Femmes Pub., 1976.

Halcomb, Ruth. *Money and the Working Ms.* Chatsworth, Cal.: Books for Better Living, 1974.

Nelson, Paula. *The Joy of Money: A Contemporary Woman's Guide to Financial Freedom.* New York: Stein & Day, 1975.

Porter, Sylvia. *Sylvia Porter's New Money Book.* Garden City, N.Y.: Doubleday, 1979.

Quinn, Jane Bryant. *Everyone's Money Book.* New York: Delacorte Press, 1979.

Rogers, Mary, and Nancy Joyce. *Women and Money.* New York: McGraw-Hill, 1978.

Schlayer, Mary Elizabeth, and Marilyn H. Colley. *How to Be a Financially Secure Woman.* New York: Rawson Associates, 1978.

Time Management and Organization Skills

Goldfein, Donna. *Everywoman's Guide to Time Management.* Millbrae, Cal.: Les Femmes Pub., 1977.

Lakein, Alan. *How to Get Control of Your Time and Your Life.* New York: McKay, 1973.

Pollock, Ted. *Managing Yourself Creatively.* New York: Hawthorn, 1974.

Winston, Stephanie. *Getting Organized: The Easy Way to Put Your Life in Order.* New York: Norton, 1978.

Communications Skills

Baldridge, Letitia. *The Amy Vanderbilt Complete Book of Etiquette* (rev. ed.). Garden City, N.Y.: Doubleday, 1978.

Fast, Julius. *Body Language.* New York: M. Evans & Co., 1970.

Flesh, Rudolf. *The Art of Readable Writing* (rev. ed.). New York: Harper & Row, 1974.

Ford, Charlotte. *Charlotte Ford's Book of Modern Manners*. New York: Simon and Schuster, 1979.

International Association of Business Communicators. *Without Bias: A Guidebook for Nondiscriminatory Communication*. San Francisco: IABC, 1977.

Kleinke, Chris L. *First Impressions: The Psychology of Encountering Others*. Englewood, N.J.: Prentice-Hall, 1975.

Lakoff, Robin. *Language and Woman's Place*. New York: Harper & Row, 1975.

Linver, Sandy. *Speak Easy*. New York: Summit Books, 1978.

Shurter, Robert L. *Effective Letters in Business* (2nd ed.). New York: McGraw-Hill, 1954.

Stone, Janet, and Jane Backner. *Speaking Up*. New York: McGraw-Hill, 1977.

Strunk, William, and E. B. White. *The Elements of Style*. New York: Macmillan, 1978.

Welch, Mary Scott. *Networking: The Great New Way for Women to Get Ahead*. New York: Harcourt Brace Jovanovich, 1980.

Zimbardo, Philip. *Shyness: What It is, What to Do About It*. Reading, Mass.: Addison-Wesley, 1977.

For Working Mothers

Brown, Susan, and Pat Kornhauser. *Working Parents: How to Be Happy with Your Child*. Atlanta: Humanics, 1977.

Calahan, Sidney Cornelia. *The Working Mother*. New York: Macmillan, 1971.

Curtis, Jean. *Working Mothers*. Garden City, N.Y.: Doubleday, 1976.

Mitchell, Grace. *The Day Care Book: A Guide for Working Parents to Help Them Find the Best Possible Day Care for Their Children*. New York: Stein & Day, 1979.

Norris, Gloria, and Jo Ann Miller. *The Working Mother's Complete Handbook: Everything You Need to Know to Succeed on the Job and at Home*. New York: Dutton, 1979.

Price, Jane. *How to Have a Child and Keep Your Job: A Candid Guide for Working Parents*. New York: St. Martin's Press, 1979.

Radl, Shirley. *How to Be a Mother and a Person Too*. New York: Rawson Wade, 1979.

For the Returning Woman

Berman, Eleanor. *Re-Entering*. New York: Crown, 1980.

Mouat, Lucia. *Back to Business: A Woman's Guide to Re-Entering the Job Market*. New York: Sovereign, 1979.

Zimmeth, Mary. *The Woman's Guide to Re-Entry Employment*. Mankato, Minn.: Minnesota Scholarly Press, 1979.